THE ROBOT BOOK

THE ROBOT BOOK

BUILD & CONTROL ⚡20⚡ ELECTRIC GIZMOS, MOVING MACHINES, AND HACKED TOYS

BOBBY MERCER

CHICAGO
REVIEW
PRESS

Published by Chicago Review Press, Incorporated
814 North Franklin Street
Chicago, Illinois 60610
ISBN 978-1-55652-407-3

Library of Congress Cataloging-in-Publication Data
Mercer, Bobby, 1961- author.
   The Robot book : build and control 20 electric gizmos, machines, and hacked toys / Bobby Mercer.
        pages cm. — (Science in motion)
   Summary: "The 20 easy-to-build robots in this project book can be constructed for little or not cost using common household objects and repurposed materials."
— Provided by publisher.
   Audience: Ages 9+
   ISBN 978-1-55652-407-3 (trade paper)
   1. Robots—Juvenile literature. 2. Robotics—Juvenile literature. 3. Personal robotics—Juvenile literature. I. Title. II. Series: Science in motion (Chicago Review Press)

   TJ211.2.M47 2014
   629.8'92—dc23

                                                           2014015327

Cover design: Andrew Brozyna, AJB Design, Inc.
Interior design: Rattray Design
Photo credits: Bobby Mercer
Printed in the United States of America
5 4 3 2 1

To Team Science and all the amazing teachers at PCHS.

ACKNOWLEDGMENTS

BOOKS DON'T HAPPEN WITHOUT GREAT PEOPLE. Thanks to all the people who helped turn an idea for *The Robot Book* into a reality. Kathy Green for being a great agent. Jerome Pohlen and the creative people at Chicago Review Press for making it look great.

Thanks to my wonderful family. Michele, you are amazing. Nicole and Jordan, for helping me build most of the activities in this book. Although it is impossible to list them all, a special thanks to all the great people I work with.

CONTENTS

INTRODUCTION

BUILDING ROBOTS SHOULD BE FUN. Hacking old electronics and repurposing them is a start to something more complex. Making robots—or *bots* for short—should be a creative and educational experience.

The activities in this book will help you get your feet wet in the robot world. You will learn the basics of electronics and how simple robots function. You will make things move, shake, and walk. Programming and building more complex robots are tasks for the future—you will have to do much more work before you can create a robot to clean your room or do your homework.

This book starts with simple vibration bots. Vibration bots use motors to make them move. Next, you will learn how to hack old toys and give them new life as your own personal robots. Finally, the book will give you some hints on where to go next if you love robotics.

Science should be fun and rewarding, and experimentation is the key. Always start with a plan, but realize that trial and error also can be valuable. Don't be afraid to modify and change the plans in this book to make your own, unique robots. Have a blast and enjoy.

Now it's time to get started!

⚡ 1 ⚡

GETTING STARTED

WHAT IS A ROBOT?

A robot is any machine that is designed to do a task. Robots can range from robotic welders to Watson. Robotic welders and other industrial robots repeat the same task thousands of times a day, saving humans from backbreaking labor. Watson is a thinking machine created by IBM that in 2011 beat two of the greatest *Jeopardy* players of all time.

The word *robot* was first used in a play by the Czech playwright Karel Čapek in 1920. He and his brother derived the word from *robota*, a Czech word meaning "hard work." In his play, the robots looked more like C-3PO than the robots you will be building.

SAFETY

Electricity can hurt you. It needs to be treated with respect. You should always get an adult's permission to take apart any electronic device. Explain to the adult what you want to do and what you need from the broken toy, cell phone, toothbrush, or other device. **NEVER take apart any electronic device that has a video monitor.**

When taking apart anything electronic, even if it is broken, remove the battery. If it has a cord, cut off the cord first.

Soldering

Most of the bots in this book can be built using electrical tape for the wire connections. But to make robots more permanent, soldering is a must. Any good future robot builder needs to learn how to solder electrical joints.

Metals conduct electricity. Solder is a soft metal that melts easily with heat. When solder is melted between two exposed wires, it creates a permanent electrical connection. Soldering irons create the heat needed to melt the solder, but they are dangerous. **You must get adult help and permission to solder.**

Soldering takes practice, and you must follow safety precautions. Read and follow the directions that came with your soldering iron. Never touch the tip of a soldering iron—it will be very hot. You should solder only in a well-ventilated area, since the heat creates nasty fumes. Always solder on a surface that is not flammable. Keep paper away from the soldering iron. Many soldering iron kits come with a stand that holds the hot iron. If you are going to do many electronic projects, I highly recommend buying a soldering kit with a stand.

Another great accessory for soldering is a Third Hand to hold your piece in place. A Third Hand is available at any electronics or hobby store. This great device has at least three bendable arms and usually a magnifying glass. You can clip any piece you are working on onto the arms. This gives you two free hands—your hands—to hold the solder and the soldering gun.

Make sure you get permission from an adult before soldering. But again, almost all of the bots in this book can be built without using a soldering iron.

Where to Get Parts

This book focuses on simple robots, but you'll still need parts to make your robots get up and go. Commercial robot kits are available from LEGO, K'NEX, and other sources, but building simple bots using parts you may already have is more exciting.

Never throw out toys, computer parts, or even dead cell phones or toothbrushes without scavenging parts first. (Remember to get adult permission and help before you start taking anything apart.) Save any gears, motors, pulleys, belts, wheels, switches, lights, and battery holders. Also, keep any wire you find. Create a robot junk box for all the cool parts you scavenge.

Electronic toys that no longer work are great sources for parts. A few of the projects in this book use repurposed old toys for bots. You can also find cheap toys at thrift stores that cost less than two or three dollars each. As you take them apart, think about creative uses for their parts.

Even if your toy doesn't match the one shown in a project, you can use it to create your own robot and give it an original name like Jessica's Dazzling Dino-Bot or Max the Motor-Bot.

Parts of a Robot

Moving robots need a source of motion, and to create motion, they need a motor. The first several projects in this book—vibration bots and walking bots—are powered by simple, small motors. Electric motors are found in many common devices. Dead cell phones are a great source of very small vibration motors. Small hobby motors are found in battery-operated cars. An old computer CD drive has a motor that easily can be powered by a 9V battery. Disposable vibrating toothbrushes also have motors, and many toys have wind-up motors. Of course, you can always buy motors at electronics stores or hobby stores.

Having a motor to power your robot is essential, but you also have to get the motion to the ground to make your robot move. That means your robot will sometimes need some type of wheels or legs. Old toys are a great source for wheels, but you can also buy wheels from hobby and craft stores. Most vibration bots, or vibrots, don't even need legs, making them easy and cheap to build.

You also need wire to build a robot. Keep any wire you find in broken electronics. You can also buy a spool of wire at a hobby, electronics, or hardware store. Another good investment is a set of wire strippers. Wire strippers allow you to easily strip the protective insulation off wires you are trying to join. Wire strippers are available at electronics, hardware, and dollar stores.

Switches can help you easily control the electric circuits that power your robots. A simple switch breaks the flow of electricity and gives you more control over your device. Switches are found in many types of toys and most electronics. You can also buy switches at electrical supply stores, but it is more fun to repurpose old stuff. Plus, you can save money and help the environment by reusing objects. Of course, the easiest way to turn a toy on and off is to disconnect the battery. Many of the bots in this book can be turned off that way.

Higher-end robots also contain sensors to help them "think." You can build robots that sense light and dark, and robots that sense obstacles and turn. Eventually, all robotic engineers turn to computer programs to guide their robots. I will leave that for you to investigate independently after you've completed the beginner projects from this book.

⚡ 2 ⚡
VIBRATION BOTS

THIS CHAPTER FOCUSES ON CREATING BOTS powered by vibrating motors. Everything from cell phone vibrators to dead toothbrushes to hobby motors will be used to power these easy-to-build devices.

BRUSH BOT

This simple bot uses a toothbrush head and a vibrator from a dead cell phone or pager.

The idea for this easy-to-make vibration bot was first published by Evil Mad Scientist (www.evilmadscientist.com). From that beginning, Brush Bots (or Bristle Bots) have become a robotic sensation, with many people creating their own variations.

Robot Gear

Cell phone or pager vibrator motor

Needle-nose pliers or wire cutters

Toothbrush

Double-sided tape (or tiny rolls of clear tape)

Button battery

Step 1: Remove the miniature vibration motor from a dead cell phone or pager. This motor is what causes a cell phone or pager to vibrate when put in silent mode. It is a very tiny electric motor with a weight on the end, outside the motor case. The weight is off center, so when the motor runs it vibrates. As you remove it, keep as much wire intact as possible. (You can also buy these motors at electronics or hobby stores if you don't have a dead phone or pager at hand.)

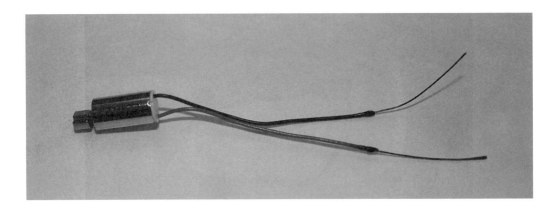

Some cell phones have a round vibration motor that looks like a small battery. This type of motor will also work, but you will usually have to solder wires to it first because it has very short lead wires. Here is a picture of the round pancake-style vibrator motor.

Step 2: Using needle-nose pliers or wire cutters, cut the head off a toothbrush. If the toothbrush has been used, make sure you wash it thoroughly first.

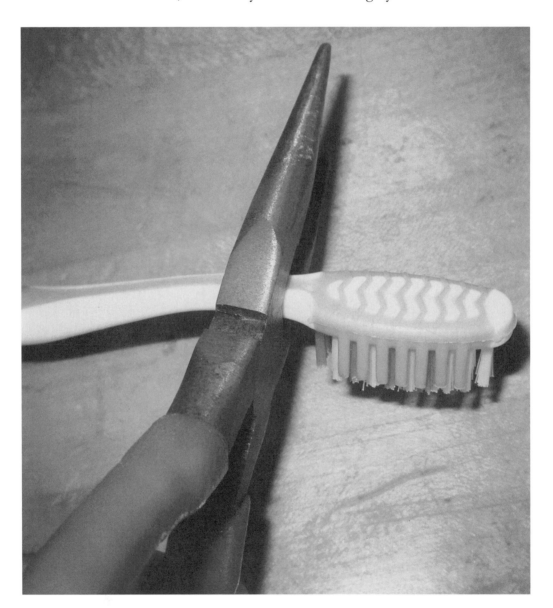

Step 3: Push the bristles of the toothbrush in one direction several times. This will slightly bend the bristles in one direction, which will help your Brush Bot vibrate in one direction instead of skittering in multiple directions.

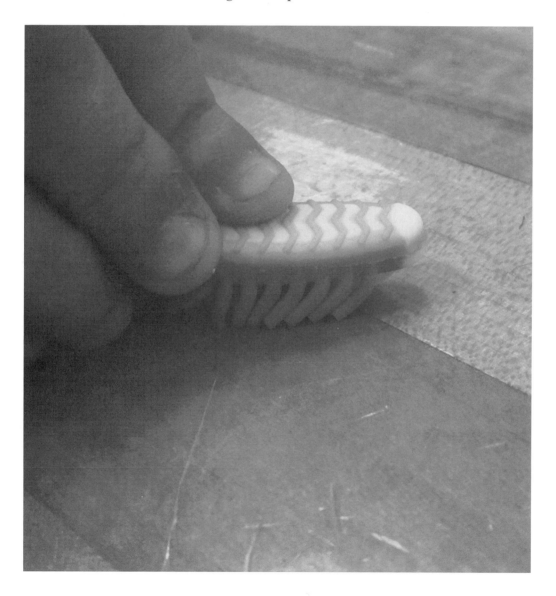

Step 4: Put a small piece of double-sided tape on the back of the toothbrush head. (You could also use a tiny roll of regular tape with the sticky side out.) Place one of the exposed wires from the motor onto the tape and press it down.

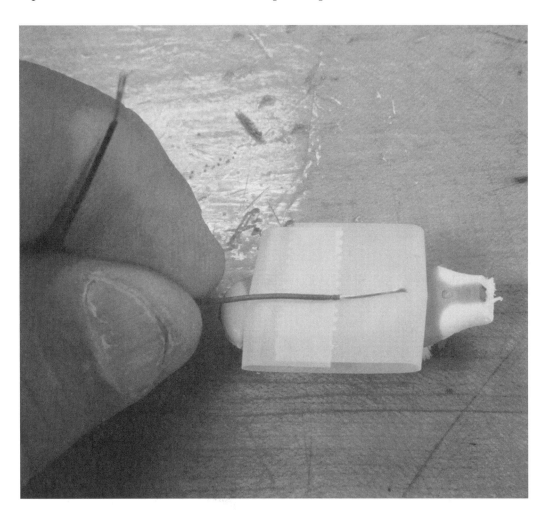

Step 5: Place a button battery on top of the wire and press it into the tape. The wire already stuck to the tape needs to be sandwiched between the motor and the tape. It does not matter which way the battery faces because the motor can spin in either direction.

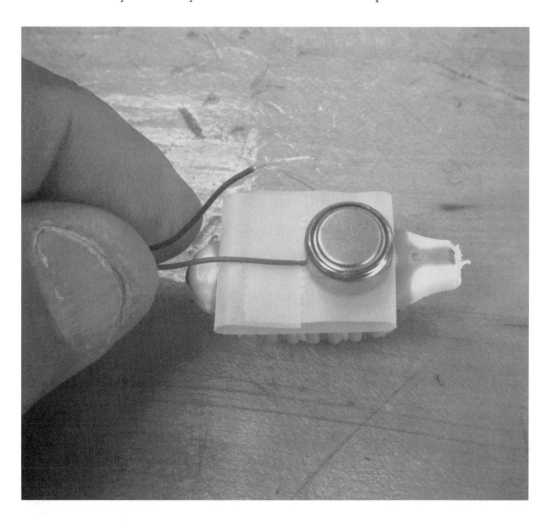

Step 6: Place the motor on top of the double-sided tape. You want the weight to slightly hang over the end of the toothbrush head. One exposed wire should be stuck to the sticky part of the tape. The other wire should be up in the air and free.

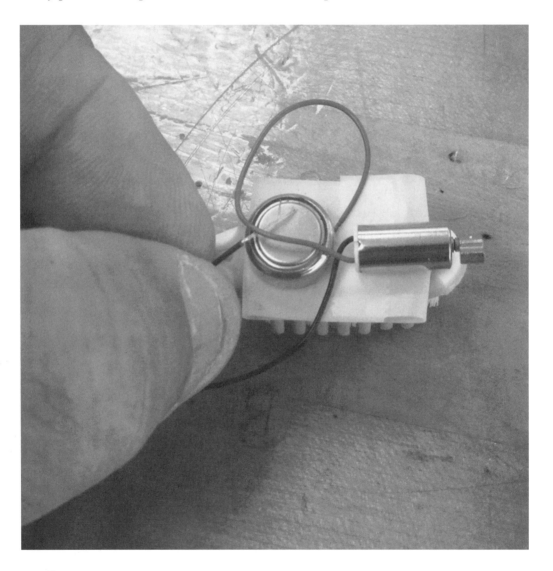

Step 7: Bend the free wire so it makes contact with the top side of the battery. Your Brush Bot should start vibrating. If not, check the wire connections. Put the vibrating robot on a smooth surface and watch it go. You can gently prod it with your fingertips to move in one direction. You may also want to use a small piece of tape to hold the top wire in place if it comes loose. But if your wire is bent down, it will probably stay on without tape. To turn off your Brush Bot, simply pick it up and disconnect the top battery wire. This will break the electric circuit.

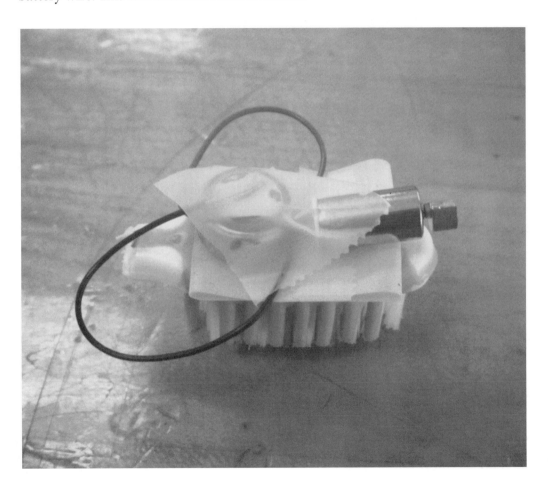

Step 8: You can add decorations to your bot if desired. Googly eyes, pipe cleaners, and strips of confetti are all good choices to give your Brush Bot its own personality.

ROBOT SCIENCE

The weight at the end of the motor is off center. This is called an *eccentric weight*. The eccentric weight causes the motor to vibrate as it spins. Normally, you don't want motors to vibrate because that wastes energy, but this vibration is useful to allow pagers and cell phones to work in silent mode. The vibration will cause your Brush Bot to vibrate and move around a tabletop.

WIND-UP BRUSH BOT

Create a very fast brush bot from an old toy car.

Robot Gear

Pull-back toy car
Screwdriver (optional)
Toothbrush
Needle-nose pliers
Double-sided tape (or tiny rolls of clear tape)

Step 1: Find a friction-powered pull-back toy car. This is the type of toy car that you pull backward and then let go to make it race ahead. The better the car works, the better your Wind-Up Brush Bot will be.

Step 2: Remove the top of the car. For a cheap plastic car like the one shown, the top just pops off. A tab is located in the front or underneath the car; press the tab in and the top comes off easily. For a higher quality pull-back car, you might need a screwdriver to remove the top.

Step 3: Remove the friction-powered motor and the rear wheels from the car's frame. You will probably need to bend back a plastic tab with a screwdriver. Take care in removing this motor and you might be able to rebuild the toy car when you are done.

Step 4: Using needle-nose pliers or wire cutters, cut the head off a toothbrush. If the toothbrush has been used, make sure you wash it thoroughly first. Tape the motor to the top of the toothbrush head. Double-sided tape or a roll of clear tape will work.

Step 5: Wind up the wheels to store energy in the friction motor. You most likely will have to do this by hand—the tape will not be strong enough to allow you to pull back the car part on the ground like when it was in original car form. Once wound, place the bot on a table or other smooth surface and let it go.

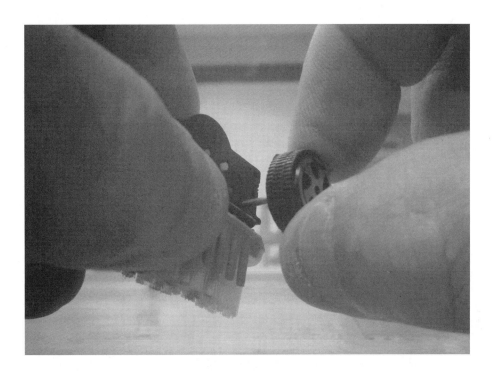

ROBOT SCIENCE

Friction motors work by storing energy. As you pull the car back on the floor, you store energy in a coiled strip of metal. When you put it down, the coiled metal unwinds and causes the car's wheels to spin. How far a Wind-Up Brush Bot moves is a function of how strong the friction motor is. Most will last only a few seconds. But they are still fun to make and don't require batteries.

BRUSH BOT EXTREME

Brush bots sometimes tip over. The Brush Bot Extreme has a simple modification, outriggers, to keep itself upright and pointed in the right direction.

Adult supervision required

ROBOT GEAR

Paper clip

Needle-nose pliers

Basic Brush Bot (see page 6)

Toothbrush

Double-sided tape

Super glue (optional)

Cell phone or pager vibrator motor

AA or AAA battery

Clear tape

Step 1: Unfold a paper clip until it forms a skinny S shape, as shown.

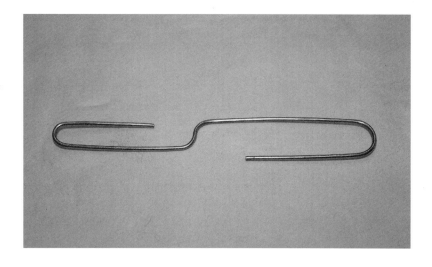

Step 2: The paper clip might break in the middle as you unfold it, but that is OK—you want two pieces anyway. Bend it back and forth to break it in half, or use needle-nose pliers to cut it. (Needle-nose pliers have a built-in wire cutter, at the rear of the opening.) You should have two strips of steel, and one will be slightly longer than the other.

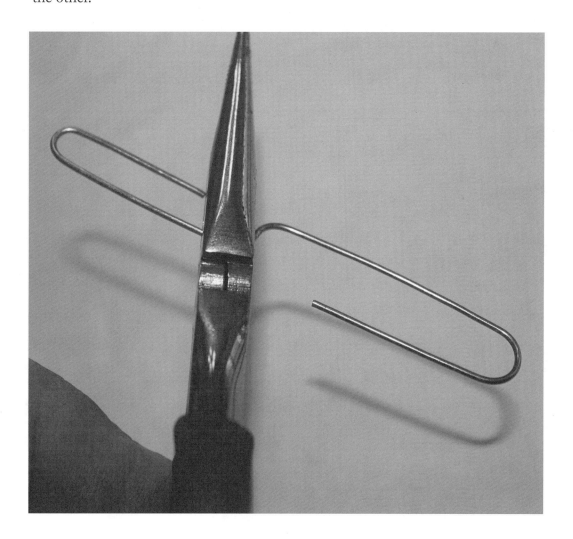

Step 3: Straighten each strip of steel with needle-nose pliers.

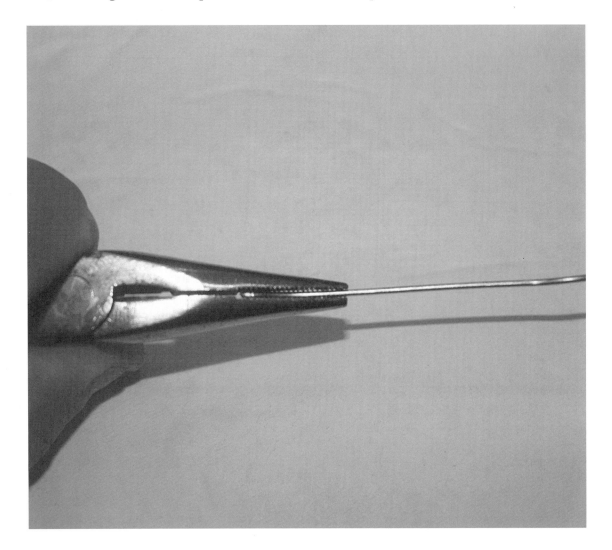

Step 4: Bend both ends of each metal strip to the height of the toothbrush head of your Brush Bot or even a tiny bit shorter than the height of the toothbrush. These metal strips are going to become outriggers to help keep your Brush Bot from tipping over.

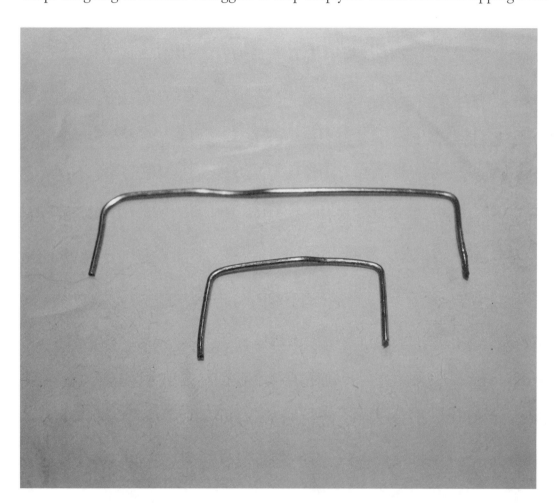

Step 5: Cut off a toothbrush head with the needle-nose pliers like you did for the original Brush Bot. (Or, you can reuse the original Brush Bot after you pull off its motor.) Place the outriggers across the top of the toothbrush head. Pull off the paper from the bottom of a piece of double-sided tape and put it over the top of the toothbrush head. For a permanent Brush Bot Extreme, add a few drops of super glue under the tape. Be sure to get adult help and permission if you plan to use super glue.

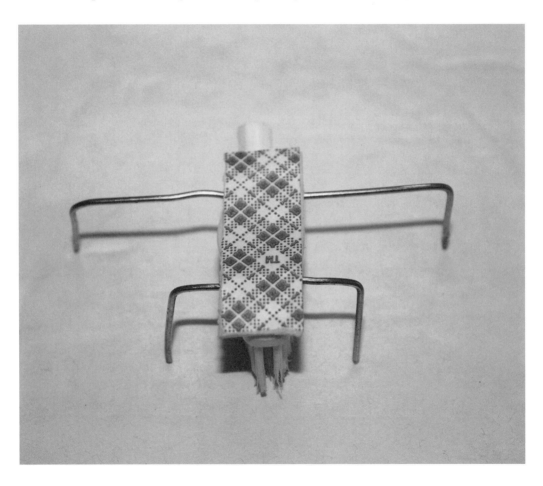

Step 6: Pull the top backing paper off of the double-sided tape. Place the motor on the front of your Brush Bot Extreme. Bend one wire back and push it into the top of the double-sided tape.

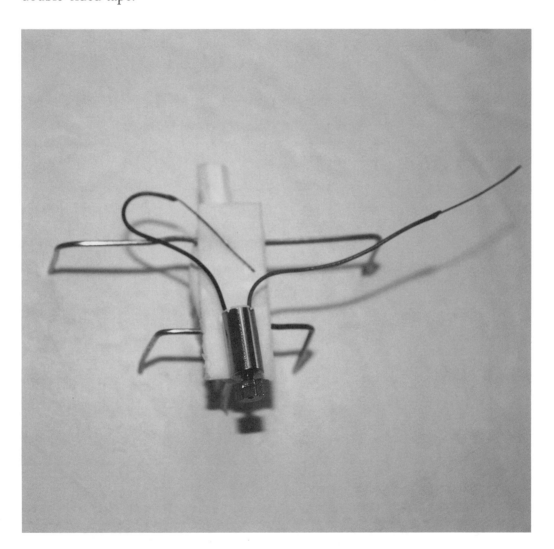

Step 7: Place the battery on top of the wire and press it down into the double-sided tape.

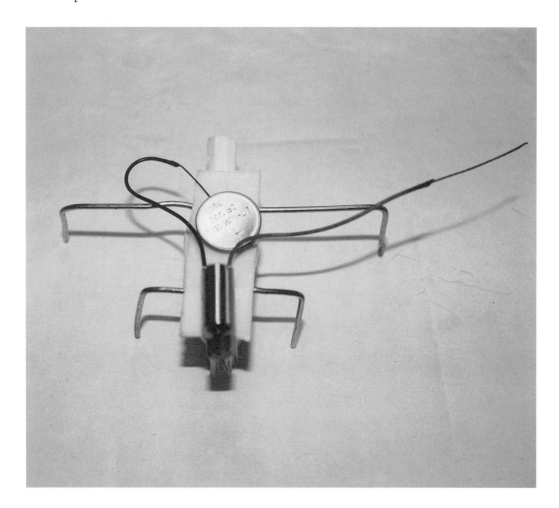

Step 8: Take a small piece of clear tape and press the other wire into the tape. Leave the tape dangling in the air.

Step 9: Pick up the Brush Bot Extreme. Press the tape and wire onto the top of the battery. Put the bot down and let it take off. You can stop it by picking it up and pulling off the top tape.

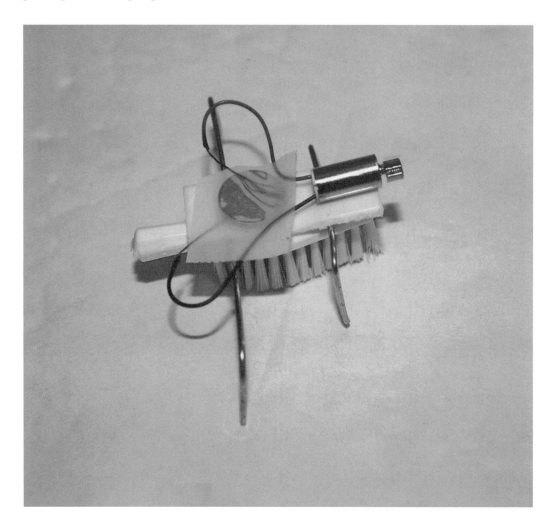

Robot Science

Brush bots can be very top-heavy depending on the size of the motors and the batteries. They can tip easily because a heavy top raises their center of gravity (COG). The COG is a point in the middle of an object where all of its mass is located. Any time the COG gets close to the edge of an object, like when the bot is shaking back and forth, the object might tip over.

Here is a quick way to demonstrate this: set a toy car on the table on its wheels. Push the top of the car sideways. It is very stable because the COG is far away from the edge of the car. Now stand the car up on the side. If you push the car it will fall over easily. The COG (inside the middle of the car) is in the same spot in both cases. But in the second case, the COG is closer to the edge of the car, so it tips easily.

By adding outriggers, you move the edge of the car away from the COG. The Brush Bot Extreme won't tip as easily because of the wide base. Cranes, bucket trucks, and many large construction vehicles use outriggers for this same reason. You can modify and add outriggers to any of your vibrots.

NAIL BOT

A larger vibration bot can be made from an old vibrating toothbrush and a fingernail brush.

Robot Gear

Needle-nose pliers or wire cutters

Disposable, battery-operated vibrating toothbrush

Tape

Fingernail brush (Note: Dollar stores are a great place to buy
a cheap toothbrush or fingernail brush)

Decorating materials (pipe cleaners, wires, markers, stickers, and googly eyes)

Step 1: Use wire cutters or pliers to cut off the toothbrush's head. You will use the remaining part of the toothbrush (its handle) as the motor.

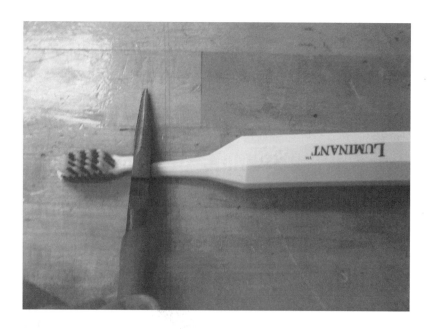

Step 2: Use a piece of tape to secure the brush motor to a fingernail brush, as shown.

Step 3: Your Nail Bot is ready to go, but add some decorations first. For example, you can use a piece of colored wire or a pipe cleaner to create eyes (or antennae). Wrap the piece of wire several times around the tapered end of the brush. Push up the wire between the nail brush and the toothbrush to hold it in place. Leave an equal amount on each end.

Step 4: Using needle-nose pliers, pinch the end of the wire and start rolling it up. Roll the wire around the end of the pliers until you get the desired length.

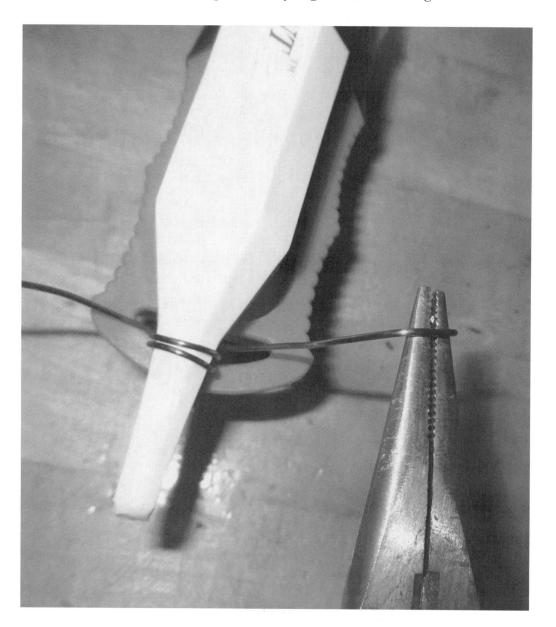

Step 5: It might be easier to slide the wire off and do the other eye. Make the eyes equal in length.

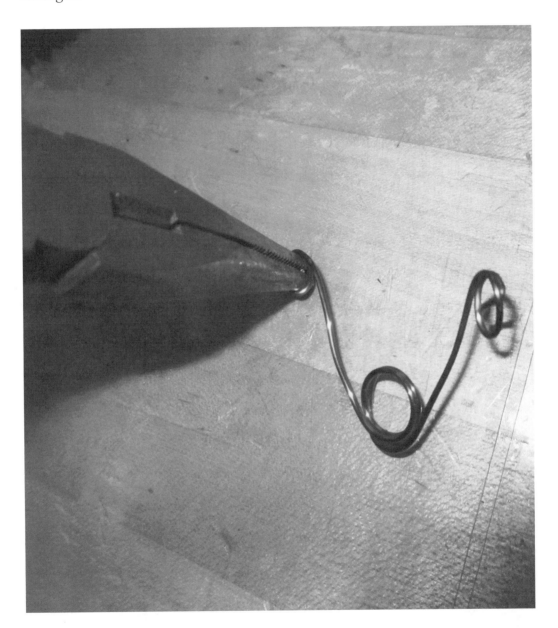

Slide the eyes back on and push them down until they are held in place between the two brush bodies.

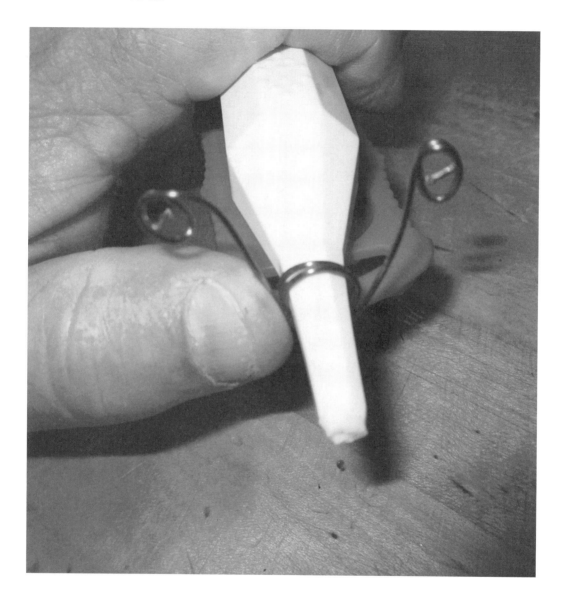

Step 7: Your finished Nail Bot is ready to go.

Step 8: Pick it up and turn it on using the switch on the brush handle. Put it down on a smooth surface and watch it go.

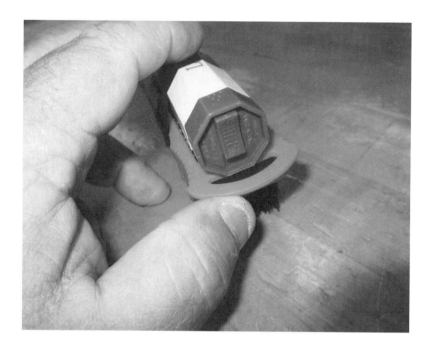

Step 9: Use your imagination to devise a different decoration style. Your Nail Bot should reflect your originality and creative flair.

ROBOT SCIENCE

This is a bigger version of a vibrot. Inside the toothbrush is a simple hobby motor. On the end of the hobby motor is an off-centered weight. As the weight spins, the toothbrush vibrates. The vibration causes the Nail Bot to "walk." You can try bending the bristles of the nail brush to get it to travel in a straighter line.

SCRUB BOT

Use a scrub brush and a motor to create this gigantic vibration bot.

Robot Gear

9V battery harness

Hobby motor

Electrical tape

Scrub brush

9V battery

Large rubber eraser (or modeling clay)

Step 1: Whenever you use a 9V battery, a snap-on battery harness comes in handy. A battery harness is a cap with two metal connectors that snap onto a 9V battery. Slide the stripped end of the battery harness through the two metal tabs on the back of the hobby motor. Hobby motors can be found in almost all motorized toys and can also be purchased at any craft, electronics, or hobby store. You can buy a 9V battery harness at an electronics or hobby store, but it is also relatively easy to take out of a broken 9V-powered toy.

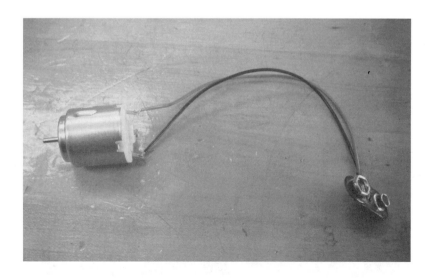

Step 2: Use a small piece of electrical tape to secure the wire end and the motor tabs together. With adult help, you could solder these connections if you choose.

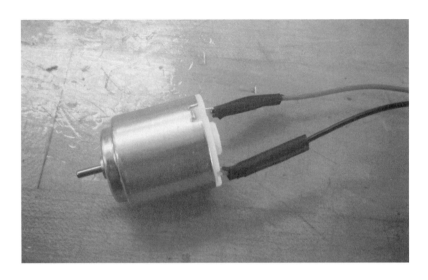

Step 3: Tape the motor to one end of the scrub brush. The scrub brush shown has a handle on top, but any large scrub brush will work. Make sure the spindle of the motor extends beyond the end of the brush so it can spin.

Step 4: Set the battery on top of the scrub brush. Turn the battery so the wires from the harness face upward. You will connect and disconnect the battery to act as a switch. If the battery is upside down, this will be more difficult.

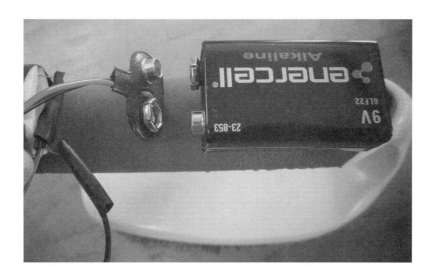

Step 5: Tape the battery to the scrub brush.

Step 6: Push a large rubber eraser onto the spindle of the motor. The eraser should be off center. You could also use modeling clay or an unused glue stick instead of the rubber eraser.

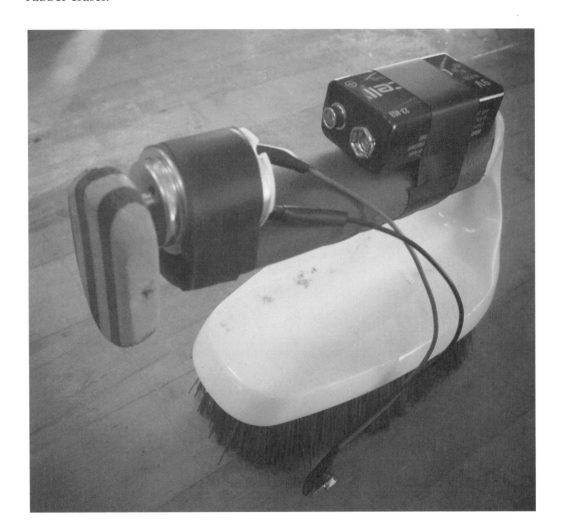

Step 7: Pick up the Scrub Bot and connect the battery. Put it down on a table or floor and watch it go. The Scrub Bot will wiggle around and dance. The eraser sometimes vibrates off after a good run. If that happens, just disconnect the battery and put it back on. If it becomes a problem, you can add a drop of super glue (with adult help) to help it stay on better. The blur in the picture is the eraser spinning as the Scrub Bot dances.

ROBOT SCIENCE

By putting the eraser off center, you are creating an eccentric (unbalanced) weight. As with most of the vibration bots, this wobbling eccentric weight causes the bot to vibrate.

TRI-COLOR BOT

Create your own artwork with this bot that colors as it moves.

Robot Gear

Clear tape
Styrofoam or plastic cup
Three felt-tip markers, in different colors
Paper
Cookie sheet with raised edges
Disposable battery-operated vibrating toothbrush
(Or use a hobby motor, battery harness, battery, and glue stick)

Step 1: Tape a marker to the side of a Styrofoam or plastic cup as shown. This is a perfect use for used drinking cups from a party if they are rinsed out and allowed to dry first.

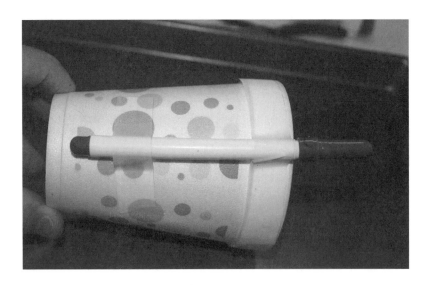

Step 2: Place the other two colored markers at an equal distance from one another around the bottom of the cup and secure them with tape. Attach the markers an equal height above the flat surface. The caps should be left on as you tape them in place.

Step 3: With the assembly standing on the marker caps, use tape to attach the toothbrush to the bottom of the cup. You could also use a hobby motor, battery harness, and a battery if you don't have an old vibrating toothbrush, and use an eraser or a glue stick for the off-centered weight.

Step 4: Place a sheet of paper on a cookie sheet that has edges to contain your Tri-Color Bot. Secure the paper's edges with a couple pieces of tape.

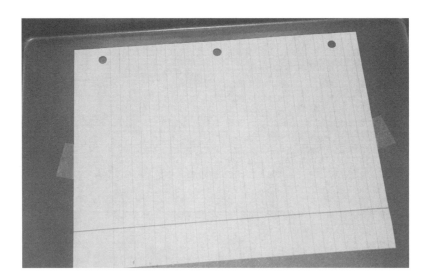

Step 5: Remove the marker caps and place the Tri-Color Bot on the paper. Turn on the vibrating motor and watch the Tri-Color Bot dance and create artwork at the same time. You can create many different designs by moving the pens. Make one pen a little longer and it will act as pivot point, creating great two-color circles. You can tap the top of the cup or lift one side of the cookie sheet to get the bot to move in a certain direction. Share your colorful robotic artwork with your friends and family.

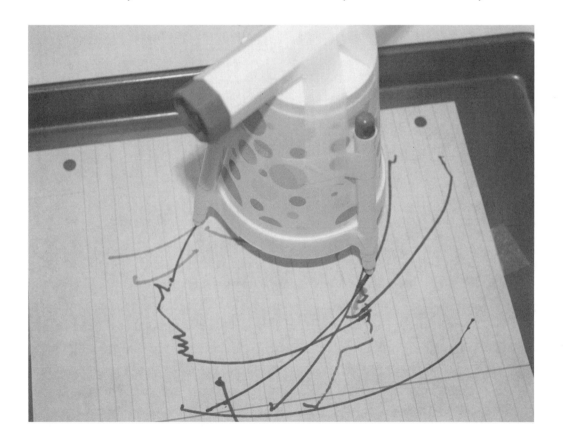

ROBOT SCIENCE

The Tri-Color Bot is another vibration bot that works with an eccentric motor. The vibration causes the Tri-Color Bot to move, and the pens create one-of-a-kind masterpieces.

QUAD-COLOR BOT

Use a computer fan to create this coloring machine.

Adult supervision required

Robot Gear

Old CPU fan from a dead computer

Needle-nose pliers or wire cutters

9V battery harness

Electrical tape or duct tape

4 felt-tip markers, in different colors

9V battery

Paper

Shoe box lid, or cookie sheet with edges

Tape

Step 1: Ask for an adult's help (and permission) for this step. Remove an old CPU fan from a dead computer. Make sure the computer is no longer usable and not plugged in. Remove the outer casing and you should see the fan. Disconnect the fan by pulling out the wiring harness. Remove the screws that hold the fan in place. Many fans are also attached to a piece of metal called a heat sink, which looks like an aluminum box with many metal fins. Remove this piece if present. Now cut off the harness using needle-nose pliers or wire cutters. Leave about 3 inches of wire on the fan.

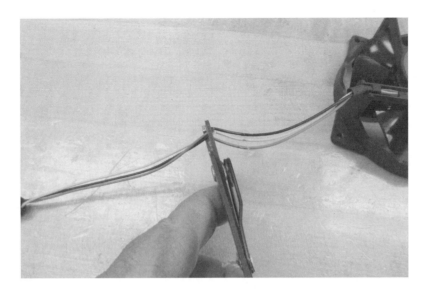

Step 2: Use wire cutters to strip ½ inch of the insulation from each wire. Gently cut through the insulation without cutting the wire. Spin the wire slightly as you cut and pull off the insulation. Don't worry if you cut the wire the first time. Stripping wire takes practice.

Step 3: Place a 9V snap-on battery harness on a 9V battery. You can buy these at any electronics or hobby store, but they are also relatively easy to take out of a broken 9V-powered toy.

Step 4: Use the needle-nose pliers to snap off a fan blade. Grab the middle of the blade with the pliers. Hold the outside of the fan housing with your other hand and pull up. The blade should snap off.

Step 5: Repeat to remove at least two more fan blades on either side of the first blade you removed.

Step 6: Twist the bare metal wire for the fan motor to the bare metal wire from the 9V battery harness. Twist the red wire with the red wire, and the black with the black. If you have an additional color of wire, just push it out of the way.

Step 7: Wrap a small piece of electrical tape around each set of twisted wires. Lay the fan on its side. Use a small strip of electrical or duct tape to tape a marker to one of the flat sides of the fan. Tape just below the cap of the marker. You want to be able to remove the cap after the Quad-Color Bot is completed. Repeat this step to attach the other three markers to the remaining flat sides of the fan.

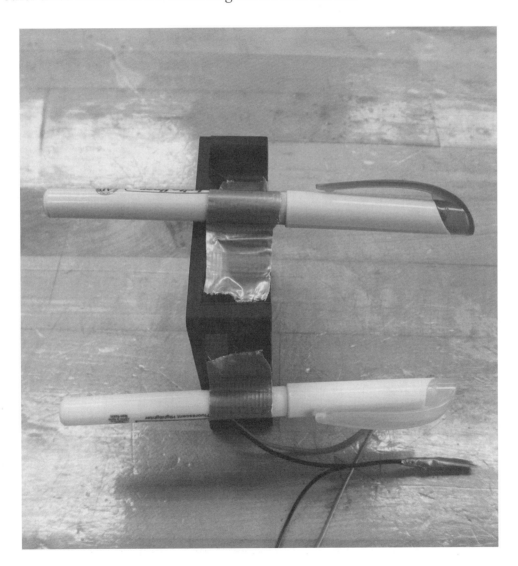

Step 8: Stand up your Quad-Color Bot. Use a small piece of tape to secure the 9V battery to the top of the fan. *Make sure the wires do not go through the fan opening.* You can test the bot now by snapping the 9V battery harness onto the battery. The fan should be off balance because of the broken blades. The fan should vibrate when connected to the battery and spinning. Disconnect the battery to turn it off.

Step 9: Tape a piece of paper inside a shoe box lid or on a cookie sheet. Take the caps off the markers and place the bot on the paper. The edges of the box or cookie sheet will prevent the Quad-Color Bot from vibrating off the paper and onto your tabletop.

Step 10: Connect the battery and let the Quad-Color Bot create some artwork. Feel free to slide the markers up and down to help it move more easily. If one pen is lower than the others, it will remain stationary and the others will create semicircles around a dot of that color. The key is to experiment to create a unique piece of art. You can change marker colors if you want. You might also want to give the Quad-Color Bot a push as it draws. To put your robot to sleep, pick it up by the fan edge and disconnect the battery.

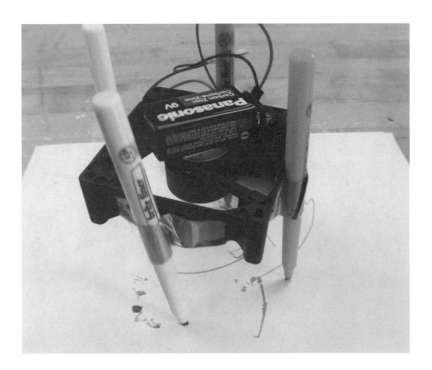

ROBOT SCIENCE

The Quad-Color Bot is a larger vibrot. Breaking off the fan blades causes the motor to become out of balance. When a motor is out of balance, it will vibrate as it spins. The same thing happens with a car tire. When the tire is out of balance, it will vibrate and waste gas. So when new tires are installed, a machine is used to add weights at the correct place on the tire rim to cause it to roll without vibrating.

SUPERHERO WADDLER

Turn an old electric toothbrush into a crazy waddling bot.

Adult supervision required

Robot Gear

Disposable, battery-operated vibrating toothbrush (Better disposable electric toothbrushes have a
rotating head; cheaper ones use a vibrating head. The rotating-head type is sold with various
superheroes, Star Wars figures, and princesses on it. Use the toothbrush before you create this
bot since you don't want to be wasteful. Once the brushes have worn out, then make a robot.)
Small screwdriver
AAA batteries
Needle-nose pliers or wire cutters
Hacksaw (optional)

Step 1: Lay down the used toothbrush on your work area.

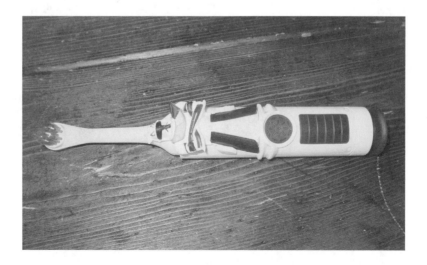

Step 2: Use a screwdriver to remove the tiny screw on the back so you can put new batteries in your dancing robot.

Step 3: Grasp the bottom of the handle and slide out the battery compartment.

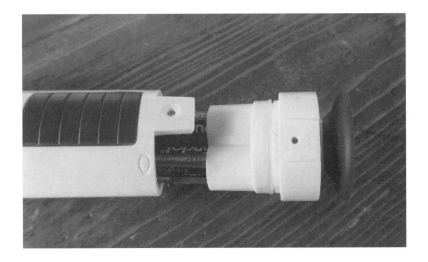

Step 4: Insert new AAA batteries. The polarity of the batteries (+ and −) will be shown inside the toothbrush casing. Make sure the polarity is correct or the toothbrush won't work.

Step 5: Use a pair of needle-nose pliers or wire cutters to cut the head off the brush, slightly above the superhero or other figure at the front of the brush. You may need adult help to cut this, especially if a hacksaw is needed to cut through the plastic. There is a metal rod in the center that you should save and not cut, so be careful and cut slowly. If you cut partway through the plastic, you can snap off the top by bending it sideways. It is OK if the metal rod gets bent. (You are going to bend it later anyway.)

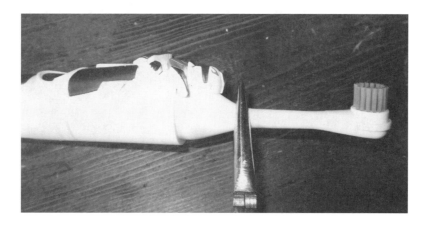

Step 6: Use the pliers to pull the metal rod out of the toothbrush head. If the metal rod stayed in the handle, just leave it and skip the next step.

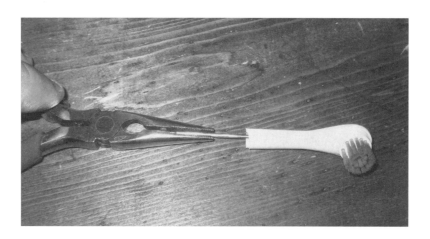

Step 7: With your hand, reinsert the metal rod into the base of the toothbrush. It has a small flat spot on the bottom that fits in a sprocket in the base, which causes it to spin. Make sure you twist the rod until the flat spot slides in. You can test it by turning the toothbrush on. The metal rod should spin. *Keep your hands away from the spinning metal rod, since it could hurt you.*

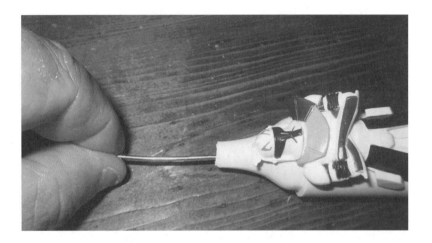

Step 8: If the rod wasn't bent while taking the head off, bend it now. Grasp the top of the metal rod with the pliers and bend it slightly in the middle.

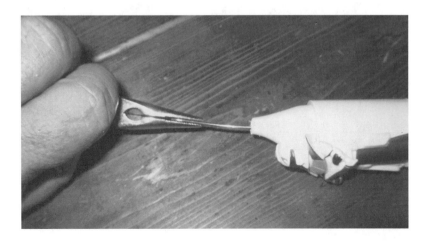

Step 9: Your Superhero Waddler is ready to dance. Stand it up on a flat surface. Turn it on and watch it dance around.

Robot Science

This vibrot works by using the motor inside. When you bend the metal rod, you are making the motor rod assembly off balance. Off-balance motors will vibrate wildly. This vibration causes the Superhero Waddler to dance.

CANCAN DANCER

Decorate this crazy bot and watch it cancan all day long.

Adult supervision required

Robot Gear

Battery holder (9V or two-AA)

Hobby motor

Electrical tape

Scissors

Paper and tape (optional)

Empty soft drink can

Clear tape (optional)

Piece of corrugated cardboard

Hot glue stick or pencil eraser

Paper clip (optional)

Decorating materials (permanent colored markers, googly eyes)

Step 1: Attach a battery holder to the hobby motor. You can use a two-AA battery holder or a 9V holder, depending on what you have. The 9V battery provides more voltage and will make the robot dance faster, but both will work. If your hobby motor already has wires attached, you can skip ahead to Step 4. If it does not, slide a wire of the battery holder through one of the terminals of your motor.

Step 2: Fold the wire over and twist it around the metal terminal of the hobby motor.

Step 3: Wrap a piece of electrical tape around the terminal to hold the wire in place. With adult help, you could solder this connection.

Step 4: This step is optional. For decorative purposes, cut a piece of paper the height of the empty soft drink can. You will wrap this piece around the can to make a decoration for the body. Use markers to create a design on the paper before you attach it to the can. Then wrap the paper around the can and secure it with tape. You could also color the paper after you attach it to the can, but that is a bit more difficult. Permanent markers are perfect since they can write on the paper skin and any tape used to secure the motor and battery. Googly eyes are also perfect since this crazy dancing machine will have the eyeballs spinning. Googly eyes are peel-and-stick or can be stuck to the paper with a glue stick or white glue.

Step 5: Cut a circle of corrugated cardboard that will fit inside the top rim of the soft drink can. This will give the motor a stable resting spot.

Step 6: Tape the motor onto the cardboard on the top of the can. Make sure the spindle of the motor extends over the side of the can. One piece of tape is enough to secure it for now.

Step 7: Use a small roll of tape to secure the battery (or battery holder) behind the motor on top of the can.

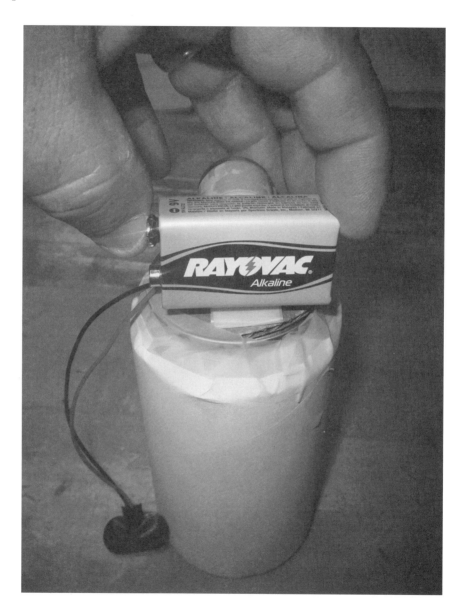

Step 8: Cut a 1-inch long piece of a glue stick. You could also use a pencil eraser if you don't have a glue stick.

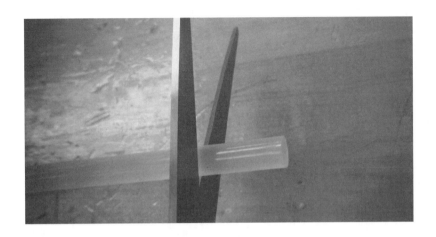

Step 9: Push the piece of glue stick onto the spindle of the motor. This takes some muscle, so feel free to get help from an older sibling or an adult. You can also use a paper clip to create a small hole first to help. Make sure the glue stick piece is free to spin.

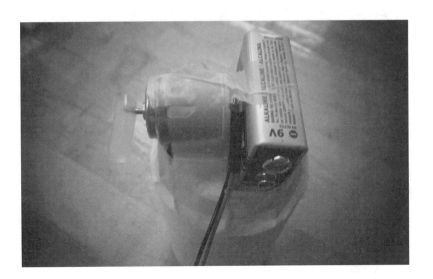

Step 10: Use extra tape to secure the motor and battery holder to the top of the can. The motor is really going to vibrate, so it must be taped securely. If it comes off during the cancan dance, simply add more tape as you replace it.

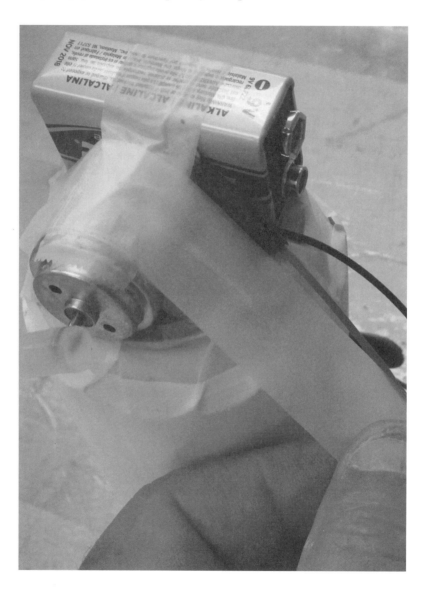

Step 11: Test the Cancan Dancer while it is up in the air. Touch the battery to the battery holder. Make sure the glue stick is free to spin. If you didn't decorate your Cancan Dancer in Step 4, you can still do so now.

Step 12: Snap the battery in and let the Cancan Dancer have fun. To turn it off, simply pick it up and disconnect the battery. As your knowledge of electronics gets better, you can add a switch to open the circuit and stop that crazy dancing.

ROBOT SCIENCE

The Cancan Dancer is another type of vibration bot. The off-center glue stick makes the can vibrate, and the vibration makes the bot dance. Challenge a friend's Cancan Dancer to a robotic dance-off.

⚡ 3 ⚡

HACKED TOY BOTS

BOTS CAN GIVE OLD TOYS NEW LIFE. Toys are entertaining, but we usually outgrow them. Turning them into amazing new bots is a great way to repurpose them and learn a little science at the same time. Also, toys often break. With electronic toys, that usually means only one part is broken. The rest of the gears, motors, lights, and wheels can still be put to great use.

You will discover a lot of ideas in this chapter. Use your imagination to get the most out of these bots. You might need to modify some of the projects if you don't have the same toy as shown in the photos. Don't worry—experimentation is the key to science— and fun.

BATH BOT

Turn an old friction racer into a superfast rolling Bath Bot!

Robot Gear

Pull-back toy car

Screwdriver

Needle-nose pliers

Toilet paper tube

Toilet paper

Craft stick, pencil, or paper clip

Clear tape

Bottle cap (2½ inches or more in diameter)

Marker

Old cereal box, pipe cleaners,
    and markers (optional)

Step 1: Find a friction-powered pull-back toy car that is slightly shorter than a toilet paper roll.

Step 2: Take the top off the car. Most have a plastic tab at the front or back that you can pry out with a screwdriver. Some might have screws to remove. You are not going to use the body, so it is OK if gets damaged. Use the needle-nose pliers to break off the bumper on the end with the friction motor. With the car on your work surface, bend the bumper away from the body of the car. It should snap off.

Step 3: Remove the nonpowered front wheels. You can usually pull one wheel off with the pliers and slide out the axle. Keep the wheel-and-axle combination in your junk box for future use if they don't get broken in the process.

Step 4: Slide the car assembly into a toilet paper tube.

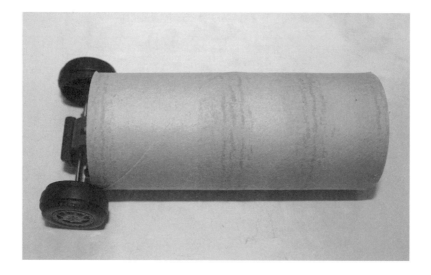

Step 5: Push toilet paper into the tube to secure the motor assembly. You want it to be tight, but the paper should not interfere with the motor itself.

Step 6: Add a craft stick to create a "third leg" to help the Bath Bot stand upright. Make sure you have the motor facing the right way. Turn the friction motor wheels by hand and make sure when you set your Bath Bot down that it leans the way you want it to. Slide the craft stick up in the tube. It should be slightly shorter than the wheels so the Bath Bot will lean a little. You could also use a pencil or paper clip if you don't have a craft stick.

Step 7: Use a piece of clear tape to hold the top of the craft stick in place.

Step 8: Find a bottle cap to act as a head for your Bath Bot. Slide the top on and leave it free to move. When your Bath Bot is moving, its head will bobble and add more realism.

Step 9: Decorate your Bath Bot with eyes and arms. A craft stick broken in half makes two great arms. You could also use pipe cleaners or cut cardboard arms from an old cereal box. With markers, you can draw eyes on your Bath Bot head and add any other decorations you want. Get creative and design the robot of your dreams.

Step 10: Add energy to your friction motor. You can turn the wheels by hand or tilt the Bath Bot and rub its wheels across a tabletop. Keep the craft stick from hitting the table by tilting your Bath Bot as you energize the motor.

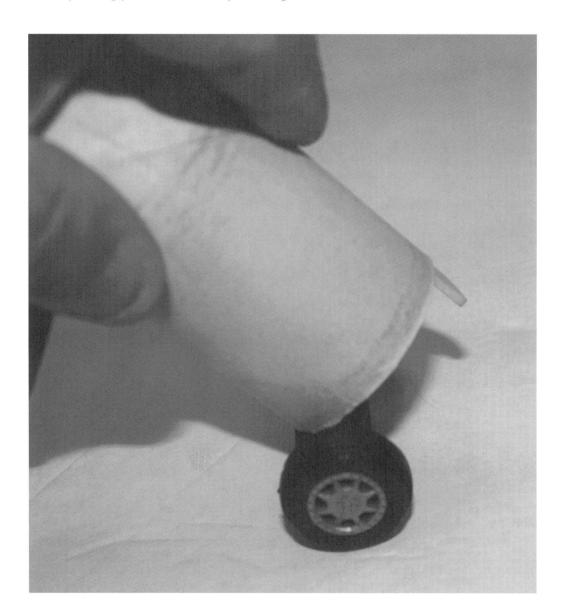

Step 11: Put down your Bath Bot and let it roll and explore.

ROBOT SCIENCE

Friction motors store energy in a coil of metal. This coil is a type of spring. As it tightens it stores elastic potential (stored) energy. When you stretch a rubber band, you are doing the same thing—storing potential energy. Releasing the rubber band converts the elastic potential energy into kinetic (motion) energy as the rubber band flies. When you put your Bath Bot down, the spring will start to unwind. As it unwinds, the spring's potential energy is turned into kinetic energy, and away your bot goes.

NOT-SO-REMOTE BOT

Hack a broken, remote-control tumbling car to create a freewheeling bot. Remote-control cars eventually break, but typically just one part is broken. With a little time and creativity, the rest of the car can be repurposed into a crazy, robot-like machine.

ROBOT GEAR

Broken remote-control car

Batteries

Screwdriver

Wire cutters

Electrical tape (optional)

Step 1: Find a broken remote-control car. The separate remote control for the one shown is missing, so it doesn't work anymore. Put fresh batteries in it and see if any part of it works. Without the remote control, it probably will not work, because the remote control acts like a switch to make all the functions work. There should also be a switch underneath the toy, but without the remote control, most likely nothing will work. *Remove the batteries from the car before continuing to avoid any shocking experiences.*

Step 2: Remove the top of the car by loosening the screws underneath. You might want to reuse the top later, so don't throw it out. After the top is loose, you will have to disconnect anything attached to the top. Pop the small lights (if present) out of the top. Try not to damage them since they might still work and can be used for a future project. You also might have to remove an antenna.

Step 3: Look at the inside of the car and see how it is held together. Don't immediately start removing screws until you have an idea of how it works.

Step 4: Remove the two nonmotorized wheels. A tumbling remote-control car will still have three wheels to run on. Locate the screws to remove the wheels and take them off. Throw the wheels in your junk box for a future project.

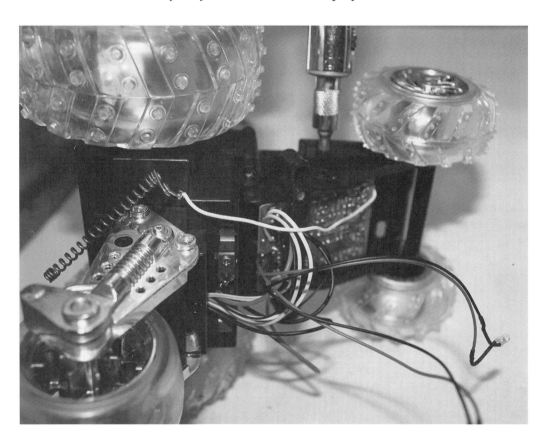

Step 5: Locate the screws needed to remove the circuit board. Take them out. If it is freed, remove the circuit board. (Without the remote control, or a broken remote control, the circuit board will not work anyway. The circuit board controls the functions of the car but is very easily broken.)

Step 6: If the circuit board is not freed, you might need to flip the car upright to find any additional screws that are keeping the circuit board in place.

Step 7: Cut any wires away from the circuit board. You can use wire cutters or probably just pull them out. Try to leave long wires on all the parts except the circuit board. Discard the circuit board or keep it as a decoration.

Step 8: Now it's time to get to the motor assembly. Tumbling remote-control cars have two separate motors in the back axle. Nontumbling remote-control cars may only have one motor. For tumbling cars, you will have to remove the third wheel. Don't lose the screws since you will replace them later.

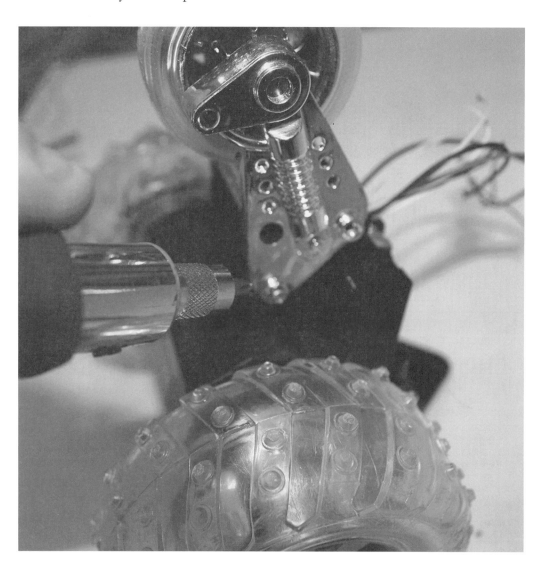

Step 9: To remove the top of the motor assembly, you will need to remove several screws in the top of the assembly. Gently tug on the cover and see if it comes loose. If it doesn't come loose, you will need to search for more screws and remove them.

Step 10: For most tumbling cars, a screw is under the wheel assembly on each side. The wheel is probably held on by a screw in the middle of the hubcap. The wheel might be a pressure fit and need to be pried off. After removing the wheel, you can get to the screw. It sometimes is possible, with a skinny screwdriver, to remove the screw without removing the tire.

Step 11: After removing the top of the motor assembly, test the motors. Strip ½ inch off the end of all thicker wires. Your car might have thin wires for lights; strip those also, if possible. The thin wires are not as important and can be difficult to strip, so you can just remove them if you choose. Test all the connections with a battery. Be prepared for the motor to spin like crazy when you try this part. Just let go of one end of the battery to stop it. Test thick wires together. Generally, one motor will have a black and a red wire, and the other motor will have yellow and white. But you could have almost any colors in your car.

You will not shock yourself by doing this next part. Touch two thick wires to both ends of the battery as shown. If a motor spins, watch which way it spins. Notice which color is attached to the positive battery end and write it down. If the motor doesn't spin, keep one wire the same and try another wire. Repeat the process until you know which wires go with which motor. Repeat for the other motor. Pay attention to the direction of spin. Label one wire from each motor as positive once you know they are spinning in the same direction.

You want to know which way the motors spin so you can decide what you want your Not-So-Remote Bot to do. If the motors spin in the same direction, the bot should go straight ahead. If the motors spin in opposite directions, your bot will spin like a tornado. Both are fun.

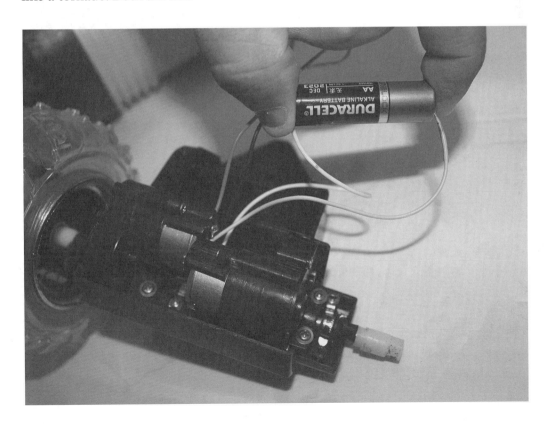

Step 12: Twist the two positive wires together if you want the car to go straight. Twist the two negative wires together.

Step 13: Slide the wires beneath the battery contacts and twist in place. You can also add a little electrical tape, but they will probably work without it as long as you can

twist them around the contacts. Don't solder the wires, because you'll want to change between a spinning machine and straight-line machine. To switch types, simply switch the wires from one motor.

Step 14: Put the batteries back in and slide them in place. Test the switch to see how well it works. If the switch works, you are ready to play. If the cheap plastic switch is broken, the motors will run as soon as you insert the batteries. You can then remove the batteries to turn off the bot.

Step 15: If the body from Step 1 looks like a robot, put it back on for decoration. If it looks like a normal car body, it might look better to leave the body off.

Step 16: Put down the Not-So-Remote Bot and let it go.

Robot Science

Remote-control cars work because the remote control sends a radio signal—or several signals—to the motor in the car. These signals tell the motors to speed up or slow down and to steer a servomotor to turn the car. The radio signal is processed through the circuit board that you removed and acts like a switch to complete the electric circuit. Electric signals are then sent to different parts of the car to make it work right.

The circuit boards are easily damaged in car crashes and by overheating. You are bypassing the circuit board and completing an electric circuit between the batteries and the motors. In this way, your Not-So-Remote Bot is given new life, even with a dead circuit board. Although it is not so remote-controlled anymore, it is still loads of fun.

U2-D2

Create your own little droid from an old remote-control car.

Adult supervision required

Robot Gear

Broken remote-control car

Screwdriver

Serrated knife

Empty plastic soft drink bottle

Saw

Permanent markers

Scissors

White spray paint

Colored electrical tape or duct tape (optional)

Clear tape

Craft stick (optional)

Step 1: Find a broken remote-control car. The one shown below is a wired remote-control car model that only has forward and reverse. A nonwired remote-control car will work just as well. You are going to remove the car's front wheels. (If you use a steerable remote-control car, just skip Step 4 and create a four-wheeled droid.)

Step 2: Turn the car over and remove the top with a screwdriver. The top is usually held on by three or four screws. They are often in a deep plastic tunnel, so a skinny screwdriver works best for this operation.

Step 3: Turn the car over and inspect the motor and any lights. If the motor or any of the electronics is attached to the top, remove them from the top. You can recycle or discard the top. You will only use the drive wheels and motor assembly.

Step 4: With adult help, cut the top off a plastic soft drink bottle as shown. Gatorade bottles work the best for U2-D2 because they have a neat shape molded into the plastic, but any small drink bottle will work. A serrated knife works well. Keep your hands well clear of the knife blade. Once the knife is into the bottle, rotate the bottle to make the cut easier.

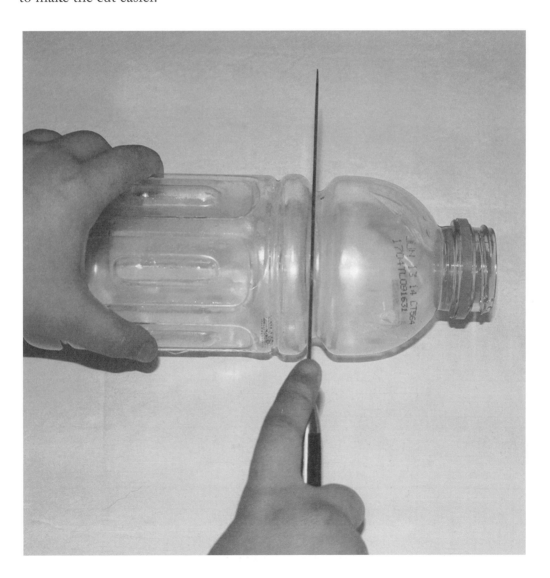

Step 5: If you have a remote-control car that you can steer, test fit the bottle bottom into the middle of the car body. Being able to steer is worth the extra two wheels. If it fits well, proceed to Step 10 to decorate U2-D2's body.

Step 6: If you have a remote-control car with only rear-wheel drive and no steering, here is the best way to make it look cool. With adult permission or help, use a saw to cut the lower body just in front of the drive wheels. A hacksaw works well for cutting plastic, but any saw will do. Take your time and let the saw teeth do the work. Make sure you don't cut any wires. Keep the front wheels and axle for future build-it-yourself toys.

Step 7: Your two-wheel–drive mechanism should look like this when finished.

Step 8: Test fit the drink bottle bottom over the drive wheel mechanism. The wheels need to turn freely. Use a marker to trace around the wheels if they rub the drink bottle.

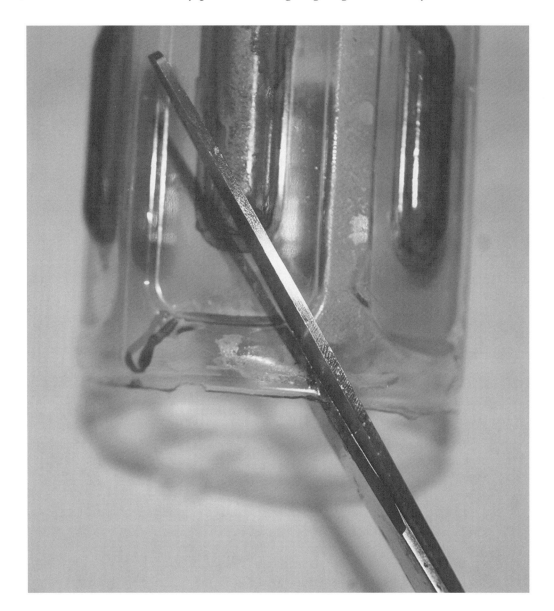

Step 10: To pay homage to the droid from *Star Wars*, use blue and white markers to color your bot, or choose your own unique color scheme. Permanent markers work well on plastic but take about 30 minutes or so to dry.

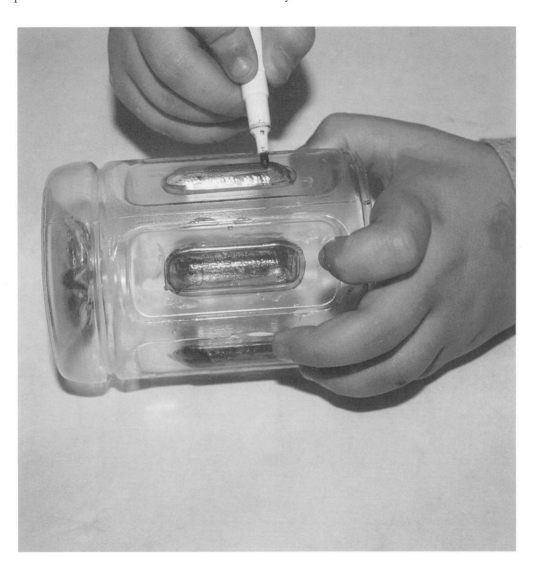

Step 11: With adult permission, go outside and spray paint the entire outside of the drink bottle. Paint over the colored parts. The permanent marker will almost always "bleed" through the white paint. Let it dry for 30 minutes before you proceed. After it is dry, you can recolor all of the shapes you made before to make them brighter if you want. (Note: It is OK if you don't want to paint the drink bottle. If you *do* want to decorate it, use permanent markers to color the entire bottle. Add squares and rectangles of other colors on top using markers or colored electrical or duct tape.)

Step 12: Turn the body upside down and place it on the wheel and motor assembly. If you left it as a four-wheel–drive vehicle, simply place the upper body where it looks the best. If your car had lights, try to tape them up inside the drink bottle if possible. Otherwise, the lights will fall to the bottom of U2-D2.

Step 13: You want U2-D2 to lean slightly like its *Star Wars* cousin. The cut back of the drink bottle can provide the third point of contact. If it is too short, tape a craft stick inside U2-D2's body to keep it at the desired angle. Now get ready to turn on the switch and drive U2-D2 into all sorts of adventures.

Robot Science

Almost all remote-control cars use direct current (DC) motors. DC comes from batteries, and the electricity only runs in one direction. That is the reason all battery-operated toys show you how to put the batteries in. The reverse lever reverses the electric current going to the motor. The motor then spins in the opposite direction, making U2-D2 run in reverse. Throw the switch again, and U2-D2 will go back to racing forward.

MINI WOBBLE BOT

Turn a toy car into a mini WALL-E.

Robot Gear

Pull-back toy car

Small screwdriver

Electrical tape

Scissors

2 pencil erasers

Paper clip (optional)

2 googly eyes

Wad of paper or Tic Tac candy (optional)

Glue (optional)

White correction fluid (Wite-Out), white paint, and/or markers (optional)

Step 1: Find a friction-powered pull-back toy car. When you pull this type of car back on the ground, it stores energy in a spring inside the car. When you let it go, it races across the floor. The car doesn't have to be expensive. The one shown came in a pack of four for one dollar.

Step 2: Take the top off the car. Most have a plastic tab at one end. Pry this plastic tab back and the top will come off. You may need a small screwdriver for some cars.

Step 3: Remove the wheels and axle that are not connected to the friction motor. Just spin the wheels and see which set spins freely. That is the set that you need to remove. Pull one wheel off and then the other wheel, and the axle should slide out. Keep the unused wheel and axle for future projects.

Step 4: Cut a 6-inch piece of electrical tape. Electrical tape is usually black and will look like the car's tires. Use a pair of scissors to split the tape lengthwise. You should end up with two very narrow strips of tape.

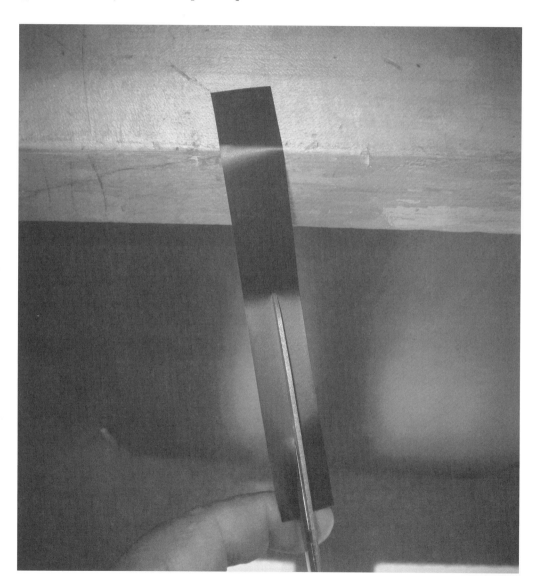

Step 5: Put a pencil eraser across the tire tread. Wrap a narrow strip of tape around the outside of the wheel to keep the eraser in place. If you don't have an eraser, you could use a small wad of paper or a small candy like a Tic Tac.

Step 6: Repeat for the other wheel, but place the eraser on the opposite side of the wheel. This will make it wobble better.

Step 7: Stand up the friction car on its rear wheels and body. Most cars will stand up by themselves. If your car doesn't stand, tape a paper clip to the back of the car to give it stability. Put two googly eyes on the front of your Mini Wobble Bot. If you don't have googly eyes, use a drop of Wite-Out or white paint to create your own eyes. After the white dries, add a dark pupil with a marker. Hold the Mini Wobble Bot in your hand and wind up one of the wheels. Stand it up on a flat surface and watch it wobble. You might need to give it a push to get it moving.

Robot Science

Friction-powered cars work off a spring-driven motor inside the car. As you pull the car back on the ground, friction causes the wheels to rotate backward. This tightens a spring in the motor and stores energy. When you let go of the car, the spring unwinds and allows your car to race across the room. The Mini Wobble Bot uses the spring's energy to move. It wobbles because of the bumps on the tires that you created.

TRANSFORM-A-BOT

Take apart an old toy to make an illuminated bot that can race around the room.

ROBOT GEAR

Old motorized toy car

Screwdrivers

Empty cereal box

Scissors

Pencil

Markers

Clear tape (optional)

Step 1: Find an old motorized toy car. Almost any toy car will work. The car shown spins in circles and moves straight before spinning again. A remote-control car could also be a good choice for this bot. If the toy car doesn't work, you might be able to fix it while it is open before creating this fun bot.

Step 2: Use a screwdriver to remove the top of the car body. There are usually screws underneath that hold on the body. You may need a small screwdriver like the type used for eyeglasses.

Step 3: Turn the car over and remove any extra pieces on the top.

Step 4: If the toy car works, you could skip this step. But you still might want to open the car to see how it works. Remove the screws that hold the motor assembly top. Be careful not to lose the screws, because you can reuse them later. A good idea is to put all the screws in a bowl as you work so they don't roll away.

Step 5: After removing the top, you can see how the car works. You can also troubleshoot it if it doesn't work. Look for loose wires, burnt plastic, or a loose motor. The car shown is broken. A piece of plastic that held the motor down onto the drive gear had snapped. Just one piece of tape made it good as new.

Step 6: If the car has lights, pop them out if possible to light up the eyes of your Transform-a-Bot. The lights might be held in by a screw. Be careful not to break the light bulb.

Step 7: Cut an empty cereal box slightly larger than the top of your car. It doesn't have to be exact since you can trim it after the artwork is completed. Using a pencil, sketch a robot face that takes up most of the cardboard. With adult permission, you can search the Internet for images of a Transformer face and even print it out.

Step 8: If your toy car had lights, use a small screwdriver to "drill" two eyeholes. You can place the eyeholes anywhere you want, but make sure the lights can reach the holes you create. Make small holes that will hold the lights in place by friction if possible.

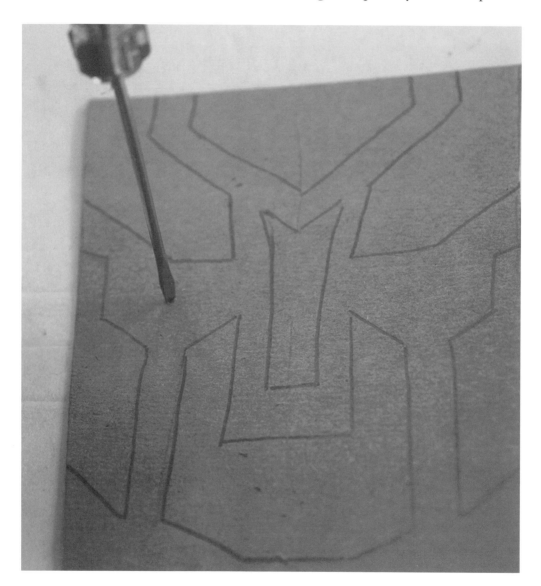

Step 9: Use markers to color in the parts of the face. Use bright colors to make your bot stand out. Or use all dark colors to create a menacing robot face.

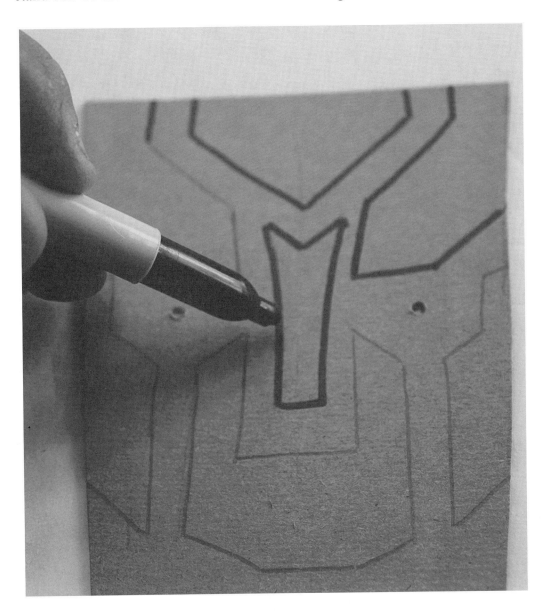

Step 10: Push the lights through the bottom of the face and center the face on the car base. Use tape to secure the body if needed. The wires from the lights may be enough to hold it in place.

Step 11: Turn your Transform-a-Bot loose on the world by sliding the switch to the on position.

ROBOT SCIENCE

The hobby motor in the car provides the motion. Inside the car, you have a complete electrical circuit. All circuits contain a power source (battery), wires, and a device (or two) to use the power. In electrical circuits, the devices that use electrical power are called *loads*. The pictured robot circuit had three loads: two light bulbs and the motor. Be creative as you look at your old toys and try to repurpose them as action-packed robots.

TRUCK BATTLE BOT

Turn a toy truck into a fearsome battling machine.

ROBOT GEAR

Four-wheel drive toy truck
Screwdriver
Electrical tape

Paper clip
Craft sticks

Step 1: Find a four-wheel–drive, battery-operated toy truck. A two-wheel–drive truck can create a rolling bot, but you need four-wheel drive to add the whirling battle bot arms.

Step 2: Use a screwdriver to remove the top of the truck. The screws will be on the underside of the body.

Step 3: After the body is removed, look at the inside. Most battery-operated trucks will contain a small circuit board at the very least. Many will also contain lights and a speaker for sound. Keep all of that for the Truck Battle Bot.

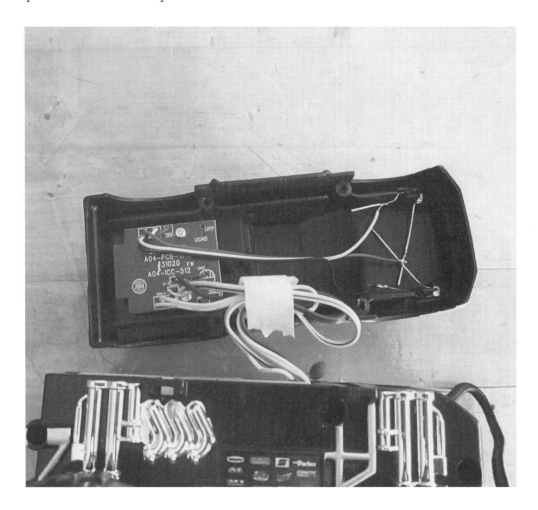

Step 4: Remove anything attached to the top body of the truck. Usually the lights and the circuit board will be attached to the top. Use care to pop out the light bulbs. Remove the circuit board if it is attached to the top body. Anything attached to the lower running part of the body can stay attached.

Step 5: Use electrical tape to secure a paper clip to the top of the running gear. This paper clip allows the truck to stand up on its rear wheels and stay balanced.

Step 6: Pull the truck headlights (if there are any) to the top of your Truck Battle Bot. Use electrical tape to secure the circuit board to the top of your bot. You can also tape down any loose wires if you want.

Step 7: Stand the Truck Battle Bot up to attach the arms. Use electrical tape to attach a craft stick to the top wheel. Make sure the craft stick doesn't hit the ground as the wheel spins. Cut the craft stick if necessary. Two strips of tape in an *X* pattern will probably be sufficient to attach the stick.

Step 8: Repeat for the other arm. You can place the arms parallel with each other or at different angles. Different angles will give you an advantage if you and a friend build twin bots and battle.

Step 9: Press the motion button on your Truck Battle Bot and let it go.

Step 10: The Truck Battle Bot in action should be a rolling, arm-spinning, battle monster. You can see the blur of the arms in the picture.

Robot Science

Four-wheel drive on a truck gives the driver a real advantage. It allows the driver to get more power to the road and safely drive through snow and mud. For your Truck Battle Bot, four-wheel drive gives you the ability to move with two wheels and spin the arms with the other wheels.

Most toy trucks contain sound, lights, and a motor, all running through one of several switches. Each switch probably controls a different function by completing an electric circuit. You can activate all switches at the same time to add light and sound to the motion of your Truck Battle Bot.

LED LIGHT SHOW

Hack a spinning top to create a crazy light explosion.

Adult supervision required

Robot Gear

Spinning top that lights up when spun fast
    enough
Screwdriver

Electric drill or screw gun
Paper clip

Step 1: Find a top that lights up after you spin it across the ground. You can usually find this type of top in dollar stores or in the cheap toy aisle in big box stores. It must have a clear top with light-emitting diode (LED) lights inside. To activate the top, hold it in your hand and run the rubber tip across a tabletop. Let it go, and it will spin and light up. You will use this type of top to create your own LED Light Show.

Step 2: Use a screwdriver to pop off the top of the top. Most tops have a tab on one side. Press on the tab to get the top to pop loose. You can put the top back together when you are done, if you don't break it.

Step 3: Look at the inside and you will see what makes it light up: several LEDs. Beneath the circuit board, there will be several small watch batteries, which provide electrical power. The electronic circuitry to control the lights is usually on the bottom of the small circuit board. You can remove the board if you want to look at it. Just be careful not to break any wires. On top of the board will be the switch that turns the lights on. The switches all look similar. The switch is a plastic box that has a spring inside. As the top spins, the spring is stretched to the outside and the switch makes contact. The lights will stay on as long as the top spins fast enough. Put the board back when you are ready to proceed with the next step.

Step 4: Use a screwdriver to pry off the rubber bottom that the top normally spins on. Keep the bottom so you can reassemble it later.

Step 5: Remove the center core of the top. With adult permission, mount the center core on an electric drill or screw gun. Turn off the lights in the room. Pull the trigger on the drill and watch the light show start. Vary the speed of the drill and watch what happens.

Step 6: To make the lights burn continuously, bypass the spring switch. Slide a paper clip beneath the plastic box with the spring switch. When the clip makes contact with both points, the lights will come on and stay on. The clip has created a short circuit, which bypasses the spring switch. On some tops, the lights will also be brighter with the paper clip in place.

Step 7: Use the drill again to activate your LED Light Show. You can reassemble the top when you're finished.

Robot Science

The LED Light Show is not technically a robot, but it sure is entertaining. LED lights are amazing little bulbs that are becoming more and more popular because they save money and electricity.

LEDs are small and can fit almost anywhere. They don't have a filament like an old-fashioned incandescent light bulb, so they don't burn out. They also don't get very hot, so they are more efficient and use less energy. They create light simply by the movement of electrons in a semiconductor material.

LEDs last thousands of times longer than incandescent light bulbs do. They even last longer than compact fluorescent light bulbs do. And although they cost more up front, because they last longer, they're less expensive in the long run. They were first used in alarm clocks around 20 years ago, but LEDs are now used in many devices. New television sets use LEDs for a sharper and brighter picture. Most traffic lights are now filled with LEDs. LED bulbs are available for almost every use imaginable, and as their cost comes down they will be in even more devices.

4

EVERYTHING ELSE BOTS

THE MORE A ROBOT MOVES, the more complex and lifelike it becomes. If you add hands, arms, and a pop-up face, your bot will look even more "human." Once your bot is up and running, you can send it through a maze to see how it performs.

JACK-IN-THE-BOT

Turn an old CD drive from a computer into a pop-up bot guaranteed to create a smile.

Adult supervision required

ROBOT GEAR

Old computer CD drive

Screwdriver

9V battery

Markers

Foam stick-on letters (optional)

2 googly eyes (optional)

Clear tape or double-sided tape

Old CD

For an optional, permanent upgrade, you will need:

Soldering iron

Switch

9V snap-on battery harness

Step 1: With adult permission, remove an old CD drive from a desktop computer. First, make sure the computer is not plugged in. Remove the wiring harness from the back. It should pull out, but you might need to squeeze it to release the tabs.

You could also ask for an old CD drive from any computer store or your school's computer lab. Many computer people have an extra one they would be happy to give you in your pursuit of science.

Step 2: Remove the bottom cover. It should have four screws on the bottom.

Step 3: Reinstall the screws to hold the circuit board in place without the bottom cover.

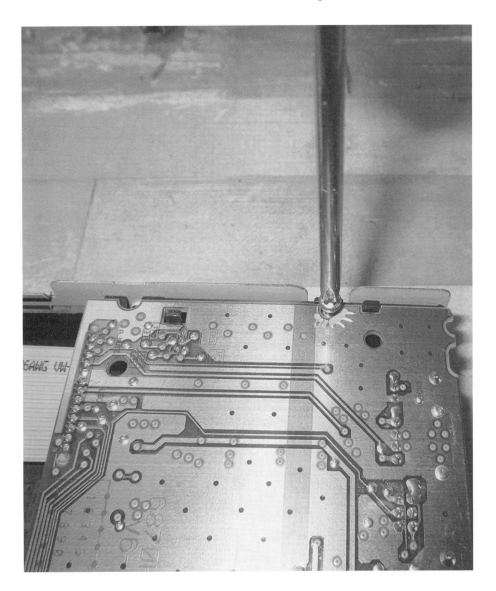

Step 4: Near the front of the drive, on the underside, you should see a round motor with two silver solder points on the bottom. This motor is the one that opens and closes the CD drawer. You should be able to touch a 9V battery to both of these terminals. The CD drawer should open. If it doesn't, turn the battery over and try again. You might need a 9V battery harness if the solder points are too close or too far apart, but I have never needed one. If you use a harness, just touch the two exposed wires to the terminals on the motor.

Step 5: Use markers to decorate an old CD. You can draw a smiley face, pirate face, or even your name in crazy letters. Foam stick-on letters and googly eyes are other good decorations.

Step 6: On the back of the CD, roll up two pieces of tape and place them on the two sides opposite the center hole. (You could also use double-sided tape.) Attach the CD inside the CD drawer; the CD drawer has an indentation where the CD sits.

Step 7: Stand up the CD drive. Touch the battery to the two motor terminals and watch your Jack-in-the-Bot pop open. Remember, you might have to flip the battery over if it doesn't work the first time. You can close the bot by reversing the battery. For an optional permanent upgrade, use a soldering iron and 9V battery harness. With adult help, solder one wire of the harness to one contact point. Solder the other wire onto the other contact point. Snap the battery into the harness to make the Jack-in-the-Bot pop open.

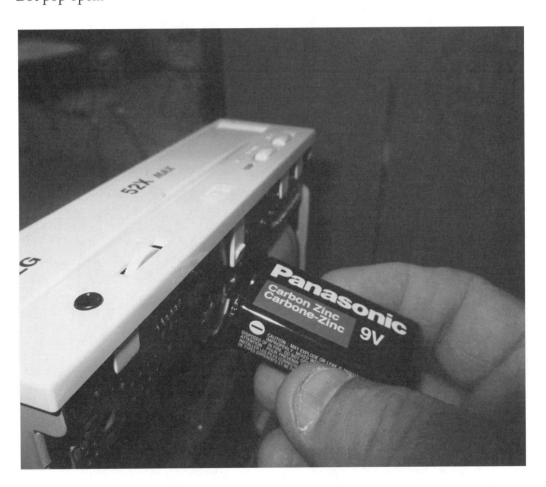

Step 8: Here is a picture of the Jack-in-the Bot in an open position. You can also decorate the metal front of the CD drive if you want. Decorate several CDs for a variety of looks. They are only taped in, so they are easy to change.

Robot Science

Most desktop computers are plugged into a wall socket. A wall socket delivers 120 volts of alternating current (AC). In a standard wall socket, the two sides change between positive and negative 60 times a second. That means electric current reverses direction in the wire very fast. AC is easier to send over a long distance, sometimes from a power plant that might be more than 100 miles away.

In a battery, one end (called a *terminal*) is always positive and the other is always negative and generates direct current (DC). In DC the electrons always move in the same direction. DC is usually used for short distances.

Even though the computer is plugged into an AC wall outlet, many of the devices inside the computer (like the disc drive motor) run off DC. The AC coming into the back of your computer is split up, lowered, and converted into DC to run many of the separate components inside the computer. The disc drive is one example of this—it runs on a DC motor. As you connect the battery to both sides, you activate the motor. This motor pushes out the tray for your CD or DVD.

FAN-TASTIC DANCING MACHINE

Turn a toy candy fan into a wacky wobbler.

Robot Gear

Battery-operated toy fan

Rubber band

3 craft sticks

Clear tape

Penny (optional)

Step 1: Find a small, battery-operated personal fan. Sometimes small fans are sold atop a small package of candy. You can also buy small personal fans at a dollar store. Pictured is a Boba Fett fan with candy in the bottom. These fan toys are made by a variety of manufacturers.

Step 2: Wrap a rubber band around the middle of the fan by the button that operates the fan. You will need to loop the rubber band several times.

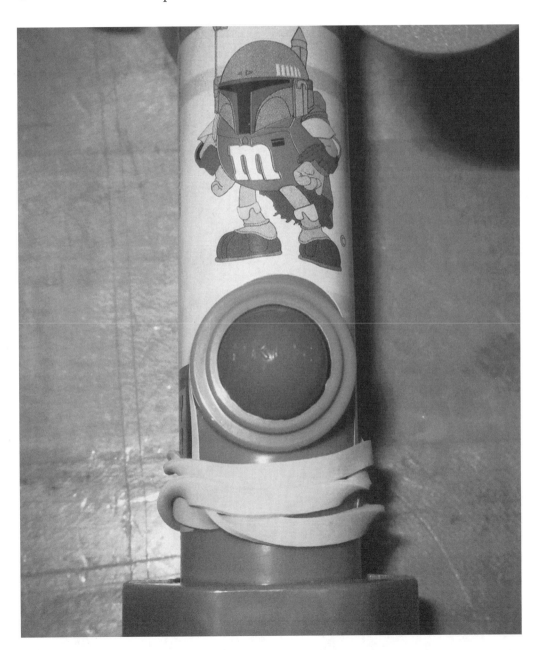

Step 3: Test the rubber band by sliding it up over the button. It should keep the fan running when you let go of the rubber band. Add or remove loops of the rubber band if needed. Slide the rubber band down once you have the tension correct.

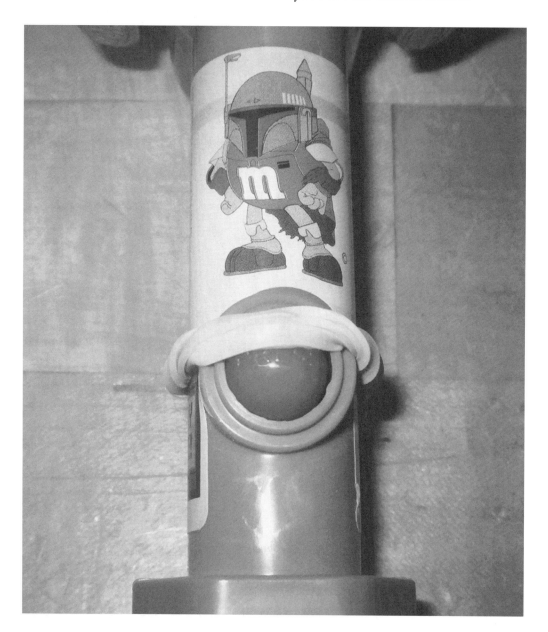

Step 4: Lay the fan down on a table so the bottom end extends over the edge of the table. Center a craft stick on the bottom and tape it in place.

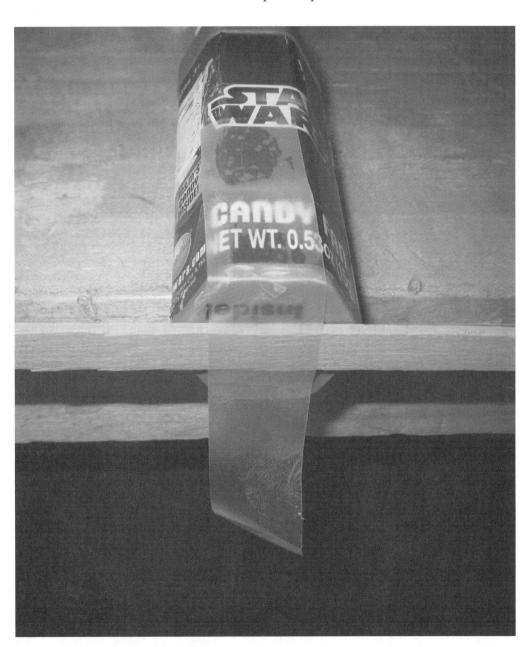

Put another craft stick across the bottom of the first. The sticks should form an equal-armed cross. Tape this stick in place by using a piece of tape 45 degrees from either stick.

Step 6: Add another piece of tape in the opposite 45-degree direction, as shown.

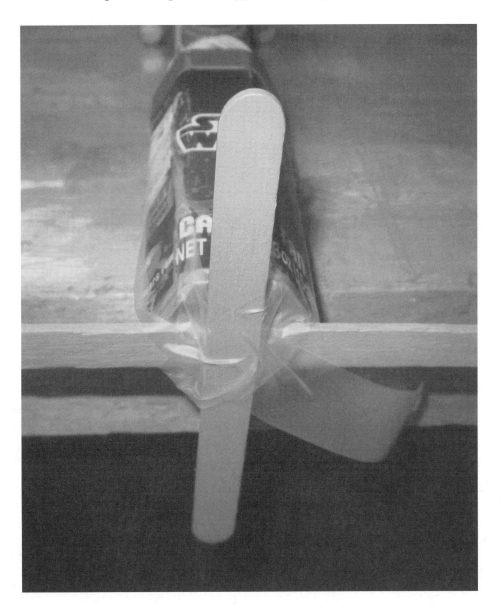

Step 7: Break two 1-inch ends off the remaining craft stick.

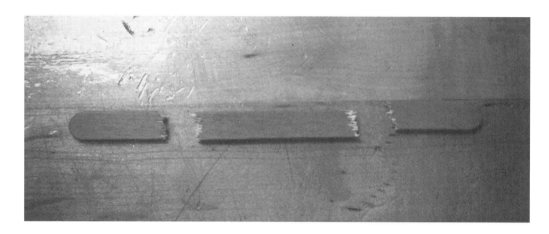

Step 8: Tape the short piece to the underside of the first craft stick you installed. This will keep all four arms of the Fan-Tastic Dancing Machine level.

Step 9: Most small fans have flexible blades. Fold one blade over and tape it to the center of the fan as shown. If the blade won't fold over, you can tape a penny to one of the fan blades.

Step 10: Turn on some music. Slide the rubber band up to turn the fan on. Put the Fan-Tastic Dancing Machine down and watch it shimmy.

Robot Science

By changing one of the fan blades, you cause the fan to be out of balance. The fan will naturally want to rotate in one direction. If it is easy to do, change a different fan blade to see the Fan-Tastic Dancing Machine dance in the opposite direction.

ARM BOT

Learn the secret to robotic arms.

Adult supervision required

Robot Gear

Drill and drill bits

Brads

Wooden craft sticks

Glue (hot glue, white glue, wood glue, or
superglue)

Long paint-stirring stick (optional)

Clear tape

Plastic drinking straw

String

Rubber bands

Step 1: Choose a drill bit that is slightly larger than the hole the brass brads will create. If you don't have brads, you can buy them in stores where office supplies are sold. With adult help, drill a hole in the end of four craft sticks. Take your time and let the drill bit do the work—craft sticks are thin and will split easily. Drill slowly and don't push on the drill. If the end of the stick splits, you can still use it for the arm part of the Arm Bot.

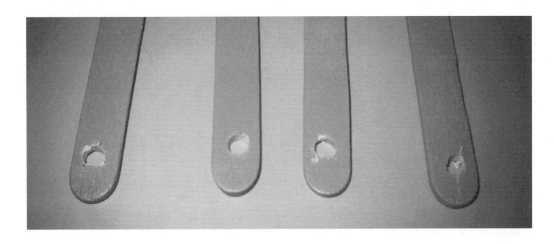

Step 2: Glue three craft sticks together to form the arm of your Arm Bot. Sandwich two craft sticks around the end of a third stick. You can use hot glue, white glue, wood glue, or superglue. Hot glue is a great choice since it is fast, but make sure you have adult permission to use it. White glue and wood glue will take at least an hour to dry before you can do future steps. Superglue works faster but can only be used with adult help. If you have a long paint-stirring stick, you can skip this step.

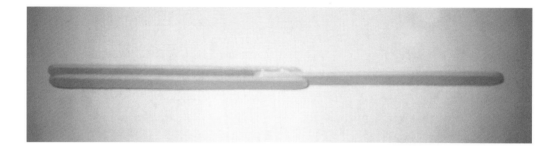

Step 3: At one end of the arm, you are going to attach a hand. To make the hand, create an *A* out of three craft sticks as shown. Glue all three contact points.

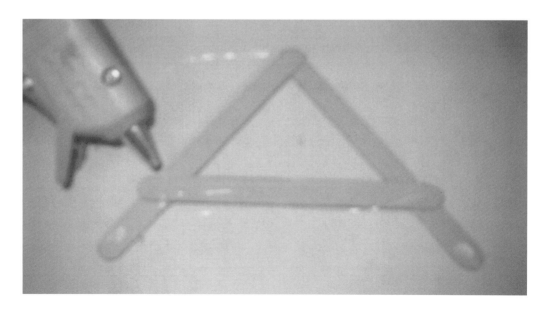

Step 4: Glue the point of the *A* to the end of the arm you built in step 1. Slide the point of the *A* between the two "sandwiched" sticks from the arm. Let all the glue dry completely before proceeding to the next step.

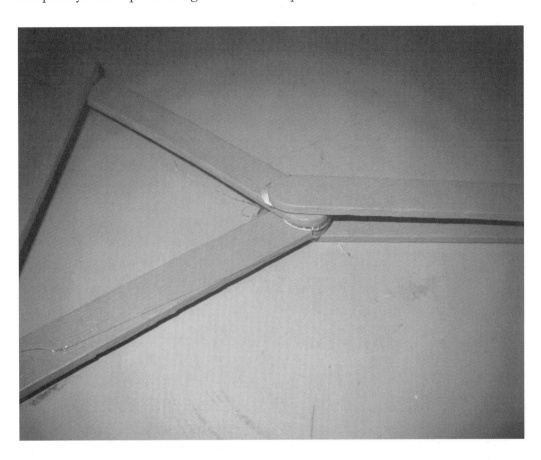

Step 5: Use a brad to join the drilled craft stick (the finger) with bottom of the *A* (the hand). Push the brad through and then spread out its legs on the other side. Repeat for the other finger.

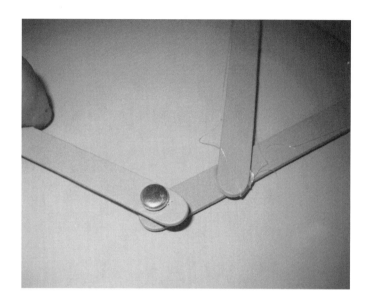

Step 6: Tape a straw to the arm of your Arm Bot as shown. You are going to run the control strings through this straw.

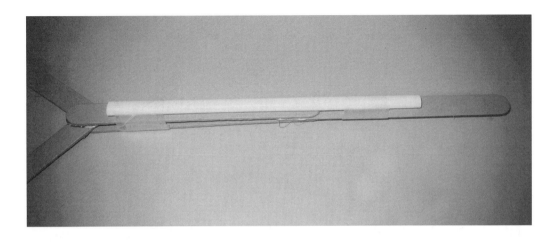

Step 7: Tape a piece of string about one-third of the way from the end of your craft stick finger. This string will allow you to "close" the finger. Slide the string through the straw. Repeat for the other finger.

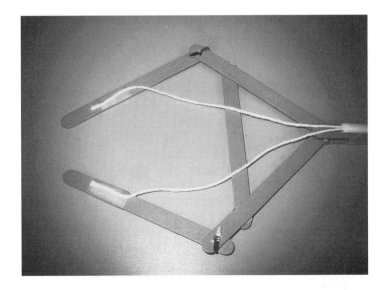

Step 8: To make the fingers work better, wrap a rubber band around the tip of each finger. The increased friction from the rubber bands will give you a stronger grip and allow you to pick up larger and heavier objects.

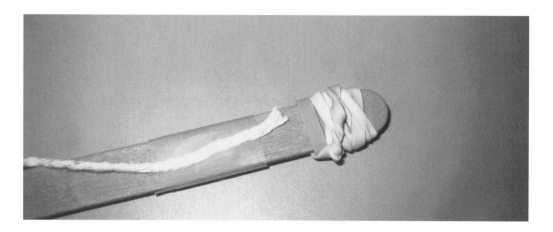

Step 9: By pulling on both strings, you should be able to close the Arm Bot's fingers and pick up light things. Building blocks, bottle caps, LEGOs, and small toys are good objects to practice with.

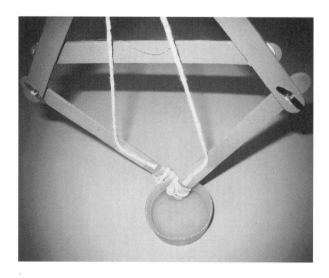

ROBOT SCIENCE

You have created a pincer arm. As you pull on the two strings, the fingers are pulled together. The fingers grasp the object you are picking up. You have to learn to control the force on the string to avoid crushing objects. Many animals have pincer arms. Lobsters, crabs, and birds of prey (like eagles) are good examples. Using your thumb and index finger to grab something is also a very simple pincer arm.

Pincer arms are probably the easiest robotic arms to make. They are great for simple tasks of grabbing objects. Many types of pincer arms are used in industrial robots and space exploration vehicles.

HANDY ANDY

Use straws and string to create a more complex robotic hand.

ROBOT GEAR

Empty cereal box

Marker

Adult helper (optional)

Scissors

Pencil

Plastic drinking straws

Clear tape

String

Step 1: Unfold a cereal box so you have a flat piece of thin cardboard. Use a marker to trace around an adult hand on the cardboard. Place the thumb out at an angle as shown. You can also make a freehand drawing of a hand on the cardboard. A larger hand makes the rest of the construction easier.

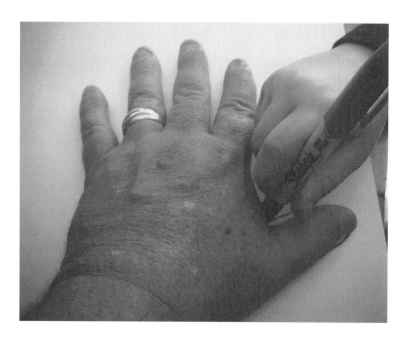

Step 2: Use scissors to cut the hand out.

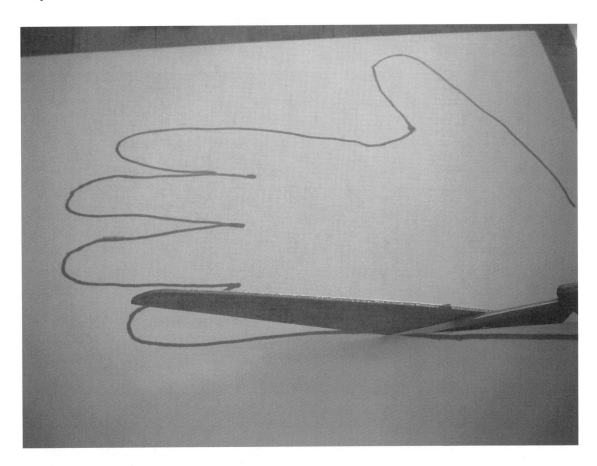

Step 3: Use a pencil to draw three joints on each finger. To make it easier, draw only two joints on the pinkie. Bend the cardboard hand at each one of the joints. Bend them back and forth several times so the joints become flexible.

Step 4: Cut tiny pieces from the drinking straws. They should be shorter than the individual finger joints. You will need one piece for each of the finger joints.

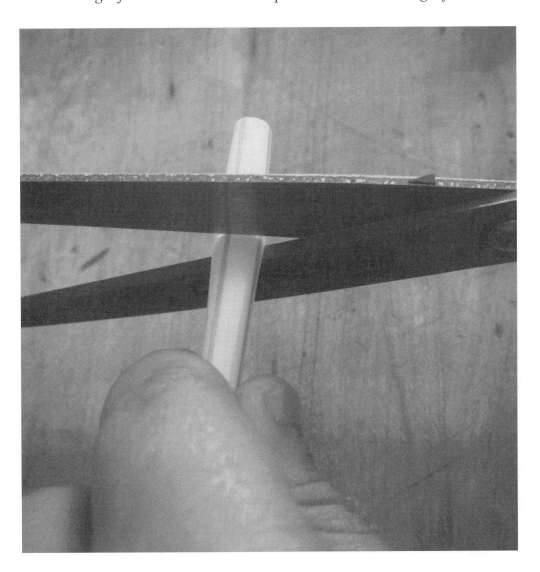

Step 5: Lay a straw piece on each finger joint. Leave them slightly separated, as shown. You can trim them to length before you tape them down. Tape them all to the cardboard hand.

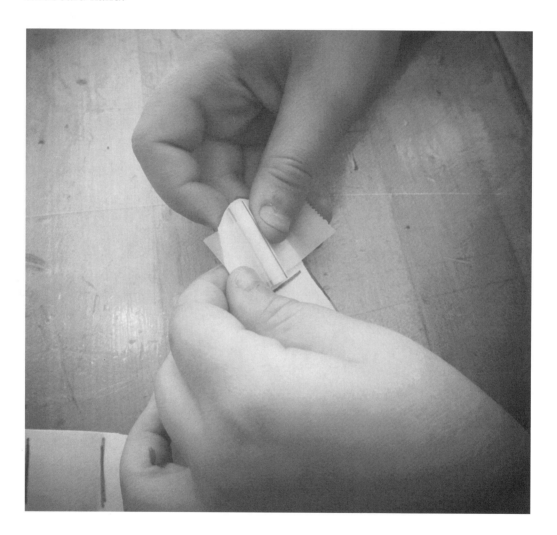

Step 6: Slide a piece of string or thread through each straw segment. You need one piece of string for each finger. Leave the string extra long now, about 24 inches long.

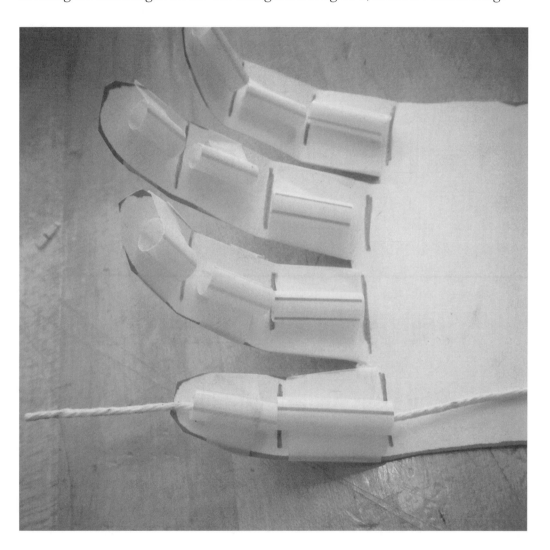

Step 7: Pull the string slightly over the tip of the finger. Use tape to secure it to the back of the fingertip.

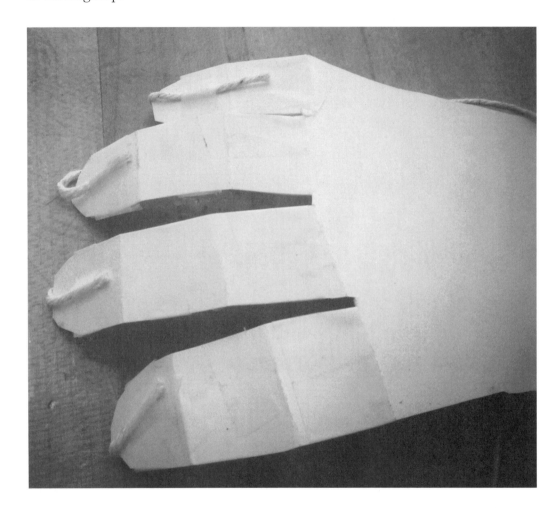

Step 8: Cut five 2-inch pieces of straw. Line four of them up with the fingers toward the bottom of the cardboard hand. Tape them in place. Slide a finger string through each one.

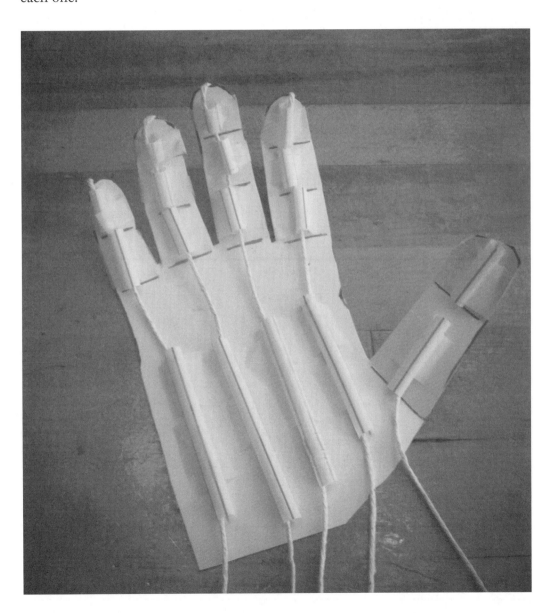

Step 9: Place the remaining piece of straw in a straight line with the thumb. Make sure it is on top of the straws that you taped down in Step 8. Tape it in place but make sure all strings can slide freely in the straws. Slide the thumb string through the straw you just taped down.

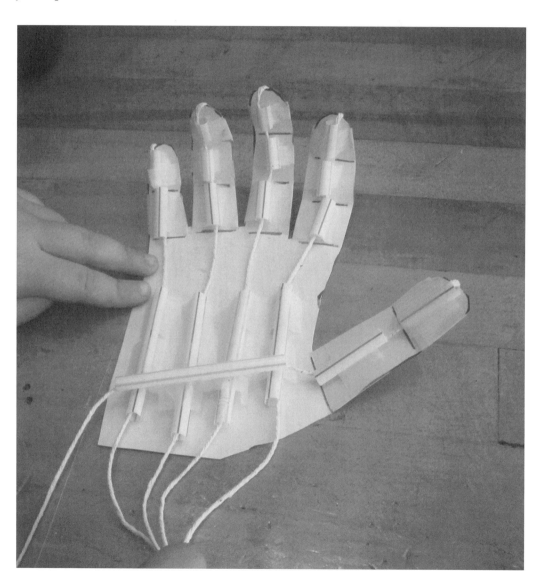

Step 10: Now you are ready to use Handy Andy. As you pull on a string, the finger should roll up to close just like your actual finger does. Pull on all five strings and your hand should ball up like a fist. To make the hand more flexible, use scissors to cut all of the cardboard finger joints. Be careful not to cut the string for each finger or you will have to replace it. You will have to pull on the fingers to straighten out the hand.

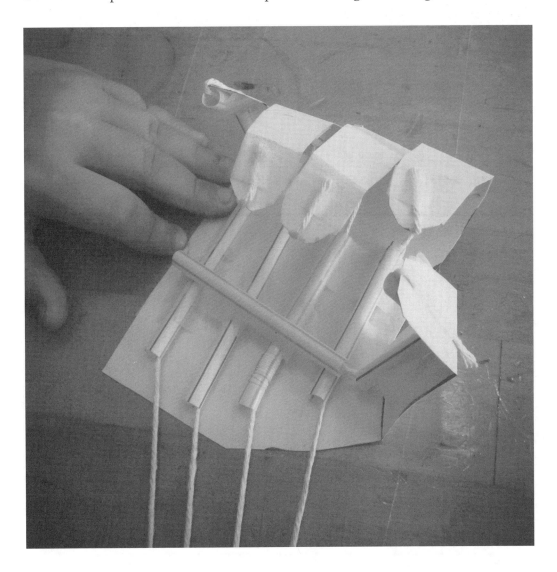

Robot Science

You have just recreated a robot hand from everyday items. The straws and cardboard represent bones, and the string represent tendons. You pulling on a string represents a muscle pulling on a tendon.

Most of the muscles that control your hand are actually in your forearm. Your hand simply isn't big enough to contain all the muscles it needs. Move your fingers while looking at your forearm, and you can see the muscles move.

Complex robot hands do the same thing Handy Andy does. However, they usually use steel cables for tendons and metal pipes to contain them. Some type of electromagnet or servomotor provides the muscle strength.

VIBROT MAZE

Create a twisting and turning path for your bots to follow.

Robot Gear

Empty cereal boxes

Ruler

Scissors

Flat surface

Clear tape

Step 1: Cut 1½-inch strips from old cereal boxes.

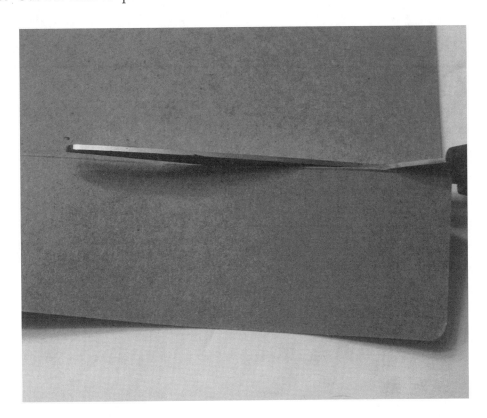

Step 2: Fold each strip in the middle. The fold doesn't have to be exactly in the middle, but you want the sides at a right angle to each other. You can use a ruler to help you form a straight line.

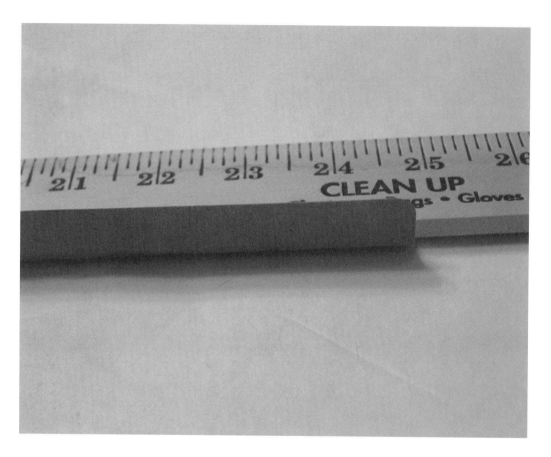

Step 3: Find a flat surface and tape two strips about 1 inch apart for a basic brush bot. Place them farther apart if you are building a maze for a larger vibration bot. For a flat surface, you can use a countertop or table. Just make sure it won't get damaged by the tape. You could also use a scrap piece of plywood or corrugated cardboard to create a maze that you could slide under your bed and keep for future bots.

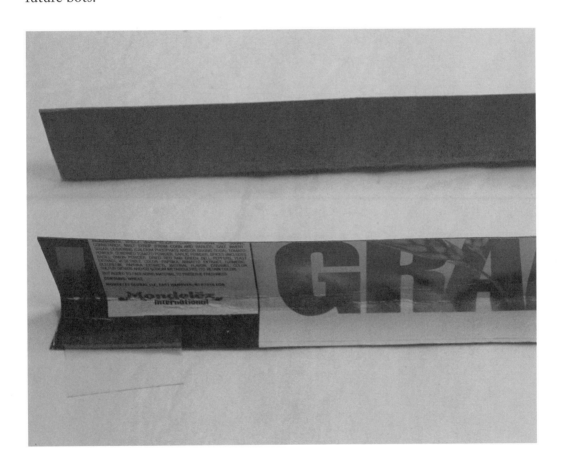

Step 4: Make some corners in your maze. You may have to trim the side pieces as you add more. Use tape to seal the corners. Corners more than 90 degrees work best for most vibrots.

Step 5: Put a vibrot at the start line and give it a push. Cheer on your vibrot and adjust the pathways if you need to. Challenge a friend's vibrot to a race.

ROBOT SCIENCE

Not much science here, just pure fun. Enjoy your vibrots as they wiggle the day away.

⚡ 5 ⚡

WHAT IS NEXT?

YOU HAVE BUILT MANY ROBOTS in this book. You learned the basics of getting things to move. The next step is to get into more complex robots that will take you farther. You will need to begin programming robots to do specific tasks. Start investigating how to make them "think."

Robots are going to become more complex in the future. They will also replace many of the routine tasks we do now. And they are going to become faster and be able to solve more difficult problems.

Robots have already taken over manufacturing. Robotic engineering and mechatronics are great careers to consider if you love robots. Robotics professionals get to spend every day building and programming ever-more complex machines—robots that may go to the bottom of the ocean or to the stars.

The National Aeronautics and Space Administration (NASA) put people on the moon, and it now specializes in putting robots on other planets. NASA has sent numerous rovers to Mars. A rover is a giant robot that can do many things a human can do. The current rover, *Curiosity*, is the size of a car and is slowly exploring Mars. It is only a matter of time until robots explore other planets and even take aim for distant stars.

This book merely scratches the surface in what you can do with robots. You have built basic robotics and begun to learn the art and science of making things do what you want. The world needs great scientists, and you are on your way to becoming one.

Robotics Websites

As always, get adult permission before surfing the Web.

www.evilmadscientist.com
The website credited with creating the first Brush Bot. Full of advanced robotic plans.

www.makezine.com
Companion website for *Make* magazine. Many advanced electronic plans can be found on this site.

www.instructables.com
Probably the best DIY website currently on the web. You can use the search engine to find instructions for almost any project you want to create.

www.sciencekids.co.nz/robots.html
A fabulous source for science experiments. The site also has a fascinating timeline of robotic history.

www.robotcafe.com
A great resource for links to websites for all things dealing with every level of robotics.

Robotics Books

Robotics: Discover the Science and Technology of the Future with 20 Projects by Kathy Ceceri, Nomad Press, 2012.

Absolute Beginner's Guide to Building Robots by Gareth Branwyn, Que Publishing, 2003.

Robot Builder's Bonanza by Gordon McComb, McGraw-Hill, 2011.

Robotics Kits and More

Robot kits are sold in high-end toy stores and hobby stores. You can buy many types of kits to do almost anything, including kits that use solar power. Although it is exciting to start from scratch, kits contain everything you need to create the desired robot. Kits can be tons of fun and educational, but some are expensive.

There are also robotic competitions. Science museums have had brush bot races. LEGO and the FIRST (For Inspiration and Recognition of Science and Technology) organization have even started a FIRST LEGO League with competitions around the world. LEGO also makes robotics kits.

Most of all, building stuff should be fun. Enjoy, tinker, and learn a little science along the way.